THE FARM TABLE

JULIUS ROBERTS

THE FARM TABLE

EBURY
PRESS

To Granny, your infectious love of cooking inspired this journey.
Every pinch from the salt pot and opening of the spice drawer reminds me of you.
We miss you dearly. Hope the food is good up there!

INTRODUCTION

It's a sharp winter morning. We're in the midst of a bitterly cold week and the fields that stretch across my window are gilded in silver frost. I can see the goats huddled in a patch of sun trying to absorb what little warmth the light has to offer, there's not a breath of wind, just the brave sound of a robin piercing the quiet like shattered glass. My window looks out across the entrance to the farm, three field maples cluster around a cattle grid banked by a rickety fence entwined in a tangle of wild roses. There's the usual mess of a farm, a dishevelled skip, a few rusty bikes and piles of fence posts leaning against an old pig ark now home to a wild cat. I can see my chickens scratching away at the frozen ground, with feathers fluffed up to protect against the cold. And looking through a network of branches, my sheep are grazing in the field ahead, their black woolly coats like coal smudges on the short green grass. There's a busy day ahead, a goat with a limp to fix, hay racks to fill, a rabbit wreaking havoc in the polytunnel and seeds to order for the year ahead.

It all started with four pigs . . . Snap, Crackle, Pop and Alby. I'd been working at London restaurant Noble Rot for just under a year and was beginning to realise that restaurant life wasn't quite what I was looking for. I loved the learning, the camaraderie and the excitement of it all, but the crushing hours, lack of sleep and stress just didn't seem sustainable. Noble Rot is one of those great restaurants where at its core the cooking is simple and all about letting quality ingredients shine. I'd always been fascinated by our head chef's constant search for new suppliers and the best produce: dayboat fish from Cornwall that would arrive taut with rigor, the veg supplier who maintained her fields and planted seeds using old machines pulled by powerful horses, and the poaching forager who always found the best mushrooms. Each morning twinkly-eyed and smiling growers would turn up with their boxes and crates of glistening produce. The juiciest tomatoes you've ever seen, trays of thorny artichokes, blue-skinned pumpkins sealed with red wax and whole lambs slowly reared on permanent organic pasture. It set a thought in motion: they're outside all day, tanned and healthy, whereas I'm here, skin a shade somewhere between yellow and grey, living off coffee and spending my day stressed to the core in a windowless kitchen.

So I formed a plan to leave the city on a mission to grow my own food and reconnect with the natural world. I'd spent much of my childhood in the country exploring the woods, hunting rabbits and building bonfires. But initially I was scared to make the leap, and so after leaving the restaurant I lingered around London for a while, unable to leave my friends and the safety of the city I'd grown up in. Eventually, and after much encouragement, I packed my bag and off I went with my dog, Loki, in tow.

I moved into my parents' cottage in Suffolk, east of London, and started private catering to make ends meet with the goal of turning our home into a smallholding. As I'd moved in the depths of January, the ground was frozen solid and too hard to begin digging or growing. Chickens don't lay through winter and didn't feel like enough of a commitment to this new way of life, but I'd heard pigs were a joy to look after. They seemed like a bold first step that would keep me rooted to this plan long enough that I wouldn't bail without giving it a proper go. So I started searching online and went to meet a lady who kept Mangalitsas, a hairy rare-breed pig famed for its dark marbled meat, which was particularly good for curing. Convinced by their joyful pigginess, I put a deposit down on four piglets that would be ready to leave in a few weeks, giving me just enough time to build a pen in the woods and get ready for their arrival.

She turned up with no trailer, just the little pigs in dog crates crammed in the back of a bashed-up Subaru. I'll never forget that piggy whiff as she opened the doors and her beaming smile when she saw the rickety home we'd built for them. We couldn't get the car close enough to the pen, which was deep in woodland at the bottom of a steep brambly hill. She said not to worry, and one by one, grabbed the piglets by their back legs and wheelbarrowed them down the hill into the pen. They kicked up such a fuss screaming at the top of their lungs, so loud you wouldn't believe it. But the second she let go and their noses realised where they'd landed, an instant calm came over them as if they'd come home. There was a smile in their eyes and a spring in their furry bottoms as strong noses dug deep into rich soil and came out black and crunching with acorns. They moved in a line ploughing through the knee-deep carpet of rusty fallen oak leaves, unearthing all manner of things.

I spent that first month glued to those pigs – and would have camped down there with them if it hadn't been so cold. They were like teenagers,

bubbling with character and individuality. I often caught them fast asleep in the morning and they'd wake with a shocked grunt as I tipped a bucket of apples into their pen. They'd play with Loki, chasing him in circles round the enclosure, craved affection and would beg to be scratched, lying beside me for hours with their eyes closed and long black lashes fluttering with happiness.

Something began to click right from the start with those wonderful pigs, a thought that had begun with the quest for great produce at the restaurant and the stories from those growers. Why are we so disconnected and distant from where our food comes from and the animals in our care? We've all grown up with nursery rhymes and a love for farm animals – they feel so familiar, but in truth their cleverness, sensitivity and character are completely glossed over. I was sitting in the pen with an overwhelming love for those pigs, awed by their individuality and intelligence, shocked at how similar they were to my dog and alarmed by the fact that one day I would have to take them to their death.

Wrestling with that knowledge was a very tricky thing. People always say, don't name your pigs – you'll get too attached, which will make it too hard at the end. But I think that's absolute nonsense. *Get* attached, love them, appreciate them and give them the absolute best life they can live. I don't disagree with eating meat, there is a food chain in life, but I do absolutely disagree with animals suffering *so* that we can eat meat. Terrified by the day to come, I delayed it for years. What really began to sadden me was the reality of now knowing just how brilliant these animals were and the misery in which most of them live. That became my mission, not to preach and shout from the rooftops, picking sides and getting into arguments online, but to show these animals for what they really are: sentient, intelligent and beautiful creatures. Documenting the love between a boy and his pigs in the hope that it would make people think twice about the way they shop and the impact that has. I think it's hard to motivate someone to stop eating meat, but persuading them to think about the meat they do eat is easy. It's all about quality, not quantity – eat less meat and with the money you save buy it from an animal that has lived a good life. If we all ate less, the impact on the planet would be significantly reduced, leaving more room for slower-growing holistic farms that exist in harmony with nature.

A love of these pigs and the lessons they were teaching me cemented the journey I was on, and four pigs quickly turned into chickens, growing veg, my first goats and a small flock of sheep. With each of these new additions

came an endless string of hard knocks, mistakes and joyful learning. I assisted my first births, watched a beloved goat mourn her stillborn baby and made the mistake of buying cheap compost that had me pulling my hair out in frustration as a carpet of weeds took over the veg patch. While initially I was very much on my own out there, I think the connection to nature and these valuable lessons in the old ways of living started to rub off on my friends and family, and before long everyone was chipping in with the weeding, mucking out pigs and enjoying fresh eggs each morning. Soon, however, my flock had outgrown our little plot. We'd always had plans to move towards family in the much lusher and pastoral west of England, and this new way of life gave us the momentum that we needed.

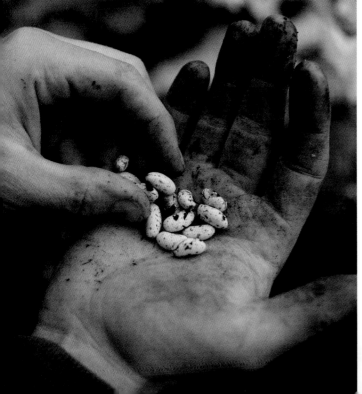

We sold the smallholding and bought a wild and dilapidated little farm in the west of England, near the coast. I moved there at the end of May, my favourite time of year, the fields an electric green with clouds of blossom billowing in every hedge. Throngs of grasshoppers leapt ahead of me as I walked through wildflower meadows alive with the hum of pollinators. I spent a month there, camping out with a few kid goats that needed bottle-feeding, exploring the land and working quickly to knock up electric fencing and plumb in water troughs so that the rest of our flock could arrive.

A hysterical palaver ensued as I moved three beehives, twelve chickens, twenty goats and thirty sheep eight hours across the country, with a few animal shelters, a little tractor and my two chicken coops in tow. After a long, bumpy journey we opened the gates of the trailer to the beehives, wrapped tightly in duvets and roaring with anger. The chickens exploded from their baskets in a flurry of feathers and immediately got to work scratching in the grasses. Then we drove the trailer up to the middle field and released the sheep and goats. I'll never forget the look of disbelief in their eyes as they clambered down the ramp into a meadow at the height of its growth. Butterflies swarmed in circles around them as they walked through luscious meadows that swallowed them up to their chins, munching on brambles and dozing in the dappled light of vast oak trees in hedges thirty metres wide that hadn't been touched for decades. And it was in this moment that I felt I'd really arrived home, sitting up on the hill watching them graze this wild new habitat with birds singing from every corner of the field and the smell of elderflower floating on the breeze. It was paradise.

The hill we live on lies in a hidden valley shaped like a teardrop bowl. The farm is impossibly steep and wild at the edges, entangled in a patchwork of rambly hedgerows, thorny scrub and thick swathes of gorse. The house sits at the bottom of the hill, surrounded by a protective cluster of trees: a few mighty oaks, a weeping willow and a tousled orchard of gnarled, lichen-covered apple, plum and quince trees. A dishevelled ha-ha (a steep ditch that separates a garden lawn from grazing land), supposed to stop sheep jumping into the garden, now provides a rather useful home for great crested newts and a stepladder for the sheep, who climb the garden wall at dawn and nibble at the flowers. Beyond this is a cluster of small fields enclosed by a wonderful network of hedgerows and woodland. The lady who lived here before us was a fierce guardian of nature, enlisting the farm under a stewardship scheme with the local wildlife trust. No chemicals or artificial fertilisers have been used on the fields for over thirty years. There have been 160 species recorded, and the meadows provide vital habitat for an array of insects, birds, foxes, voles and much more. At night, owls hoot from every corner of the farm, where she planted 2,000 trees that have now matured into broadleaf woodland, home to woodcock, woodpeckers, hawks, buzzards, badgers and a nightjar. It is a special place, and from the higher fields you look across the vale, through a tapestry of farms, to where the sea can be glimpsed between the hills of the coast. We aim to build on her legacy.

The land around us is generally home to quite intensive dairy farming, which tends to squeeze nature right to the edges, leaving little habitat for much else. Here we aim to provide a sanctuary for nature, an oasis in the desert, while also growing food. We have seeded three further fields with diverse wildflower mixes in a meadow restoration project, and will plant more trees in a bid to create an increasingly rare dynamic habitat called woodland pasture. This will provide a home for many species as well as grazing for my animals and drought resistance. My flock are all rare primitive breeds that are much smaller and slower-growing than modern breeds. They have less impact on the land, as they need little to survive, and live in harmony with nature rather than competing with it. We keep them in small numbers, rotated carefully around the fields so that the wildflower can bloom for as long as possible and set its seeds. At which point my sheep and goats trample and spread those seeds into the ground, holding back the grass over winter so the wildflower has the best chance when it grows again in spring.

It might look a bit dreamy from afar, and a lot of the time it is. On a good day this is an extraordinary way of life, waking with the sun, your day dictated by the seasons, out there in the elements, at one with nature. Even on a bad day, there's a real truth to it all, a beauty in the hard moments. Nature is tough and unforgiving. But it's also me trimming hundreds of toenails in the mud and driving rain, delivering kid goats and lambs in spring, getting my hands in when they are breeched and need pulling out. It's me on the sad days when births go wrong or an infection spreads its way through the flock or, even worse, betrayal day at the abattoir. This hasn't all just puffed out of nowhere, it's been a slow journey of eight years, building the farm and its elements little by little, learning on the fly through a series of setbacks and hard-won lessons. I've had some brilliant advice along the way and met some fantastic mentors, but really the most important things I've learnt have been through some pretty brutal mistakes.

I used to do this all by myself with occasional help from family and friends catching this or weeding that, roping in my brothers in exchange for chicken pies and ham hock stews. But things have now grown to a point where I need an extra pair of hands, and my brother Joss works with me on the farm as my right-hand man. He does much of the vegetable growing and hay-rack filling and is a master at catching lusty billy goats at all hours when they lock on to the smell of the girls in autumn. The ten goats I started with are now forty, a rare breed called the British primitive goat that I keep for conservation purposes and a love for this brilliantly curious and characterful animal. My flock of eleven Hebridean sheep is now one hundred . . . with thirty breeding ewes that give birth to about fifty lambs each year, and this will be the main source of income for our small farm. As I said, they are a slow-growing heritage breed, so I keep these lambs for about fifteen months (compared to the four-to-six-month life of commercially reared lambs), rotating them through our permanent pasture before they get sold directly to friends, family and local butchers as hogget. The abattoir always says it'll get easier, you'll get used to it . . . but I never will and never want to. I have a deep connection and love for my animals, and that day, taking them in, weighs on me for weeks before and after. It feels the utmost betrayal and I often teeter on the edge. But it is also a great privilege to know where your food comes from and the true price of it: the hours of care and careful husbandry, the relationship with the land from whence they came and the moral cost of death and what that really means.

My plan on the farm initially was to see if I could get somewhere close to self-sufficiency. While this is a nice idea, I think what I'm really doing is just trying to learn and see where it takes me. I've never had cows, and dream of making my own cheese. I'd love to have pigs again, clearing some of the bramble in the woods and creating opportunities for dynamic biodiversity and habitat-building with an animal that would once have been an intrinsic part of the environment. I often dream of planting a little patch of wheat, just to see what it really means to grow, mill, bake and eat a loaf of bread. Nothing is certain in life, but the one thing I know is that I love being rooted to the seasons and feeling connected to nature. This way of life and the learning it brings is such a privilege, and my dream would be to build a place of my own and make a home where people could come and stay and experience it for themselves, really feel like they lived there, helping with the animals, cooking together, gardening and beekeeping.

All this farming is, of course, underpinned by a great love of food. Throughout my journey, cooking has been at the core of it all; it is how I interact with the world, my way of sharing and giving. The kitchen has always been the heart of our home, where we talk, argue, discuss and deliberate. Home to dogs, sickly chickens, endless washing drying by the stove, goats that need bottle-feeding and wet lambs in need of warmth. Every corner is piled high with books, plants and an ever-growing collection of plates. It's where I spend my days and nights, pots bubbling away and pans sizzling, leaving behind a trail of mess and destruction that often has me in trouble. But . . . is there a better way to show your love for someone? The simple act of bringing a steaming pot to the table that you've poured your heart into. Bowls passed round, bread torn and buttered. The collective pleasure after that first mouthful and the hum of conversation spurred on by good, simple food. Cooking is what makes us human.

There are about 100 recipes to follow – some are more 'ways' than recipes – ideas to inspire rather than rules to follow, organised by the seasons, as that's how I believe we should be eating. While I've got a little restaurant experience under my belt, deep down I am just a home cook who loves his food, and the recipes that follow are wonderfully simple. Eating seasonally means you are eating produce at its prime and bursting with flavour. So as a cook there's not much you have to do other than keep it simple and let the flavours shine. Generally the recipes celebrate just a few good things on the plate, with a little clever seasoning.

Each season has a mix of smaller plates, veg dishes, fish and meat, with a few epic yet easy puddings to finish. But, crucially, these recipes don't have to be tied to the season that they are in. If you like something, I implore you to play with it and adapt it to the produce available around you. Spring on a plate – a delicious medley of braised spring vegetables on a bed of whipped ricotta – is one of my favourite recipes in the book (see page 118). While, yes, it is great in spring, you can absolutely change the mix of vegetables on top, adapting the recipe to the season that you are in. Try courgettes and tomatoes in summer, charred sweetcorn or roasted squash in autumn and an earthy mix of Swiss chard and cavolo nero in winter. Similarly, if something has meat in it, but you are vegetarian, just take it out. Cooking should be playful, instinctive and freeing!

If recipes are stories, this book is a collection of moments from my first three years on our little farm. It has been a time of rich exploration and inspiration, learning to really connect with the place I now call home. I hope the recipes that follow provide a window into my life here and inspire a new connection to the seasons. This is simple home cooking, made from a place of love, not only for the people eating it, but for the land it came from. Quick dishes made in an instant while kid goats climb the kitchen table and nibble at the wallpaper. Steaming bowls of soup and broth brought out to the garden while we dig the veg patch and discover the richness of the soil that feeds us through the year. It is a collection of recipes made with muddy fingernails and much to do. But also food made on slower days after long walks, really relishing the grounding act of cooking, enjoying the methodical process and the joyful dance of ingredients into the pan.

Working in the restaurant world was a deeply formative experience. I had a fascinating time, learning all sorts of technical skills, the true meaning of hard work and how to work as a team. The camaraderie of those kitchens will stay with me forever, and a little part of me has always wished I had stayed longer. It's incredible the speed of learning in a kitchen environment and I just wanted to talk about two vital lessons I took away from that world which will always be at the heart of my food: cooking seasonally and the art of seasoning.

Seasonality

Seasonality is the principle of being guided by the seasons in the way you shop and eat. Enjoying asparagus in spring, making the most of the short season by eating it almost every day, until you've had your yearly fill and are desperate for the arrival of tomatoes and courgettes in summer. Then patiently waiting, not touching a spear grown abroad until the cycle repeats and the season comes round again so you can feast on it once more. What a joy it is to miss something, anticipation building as you wait for its return. It makes veg exciting. I look forward to my first pumpkin of the year, snapping my first sweetcorn off the stalk and picking wild cherries with juice bleeding down my arm. Cooking seasonally ensures you are eating produce in its prime, when it will be at its most nutritious and most flavourful, and as a cook that makes a huge difference! In the kitchen all you can do is enhance flavour; you cannot create flavour that wasn't there in the first place. If you start with produce at its peak, half the work is already done for you and all you need to do is keep it simple to create exceptionally delicious food.

Think of a tomato at its best, a big fat bull's-heart tomato, perfectly grown and bursting with juice. It's almost a crime to do anything other than eat it with good olive oil, flaky salt and a leaf of basil or two. How sad it is to eat a flavourless tomato in the midst of winter, grown under artificial lighting, in a heated greenhouse and flown in from miles away. There's no amount of olive oil or salt that will save that, so I'd rather wait and eat something in season like cavolo nero, grown outside as nature intended and bursting with flavour.

Eating seasonally will transform your cooking, but importantly you will also be protecting our planet by buying local produce with significantly fewer (if any) air miles; it uses far less carbon, fewer chemicals and causes less damage to the environment. It's also cheaper! When things are in season they are easy to grow and therefore abundant.

Lastly, the seasons also vary greatly depending on where you are, so please don't feel you have to stick to a certain chapter, and instead feel free to adapt these recipes according to what you have around you. In our cooler climate for instance, I see tomatoes as a mid-to-late summer ingredient that we enjoy right through autumn, until the first frosts appear. But if you're somewhere warmer, you might be eating them much earlier in (what I would consider as) Spring. Because I live in England, my general rule is to live by the European seasons. If some early Italian broad beans appear in the farm shop, I'm not against starting the season before our own local produce begins to appear. Equally so, when they're in season, I make the most of beautiful ingredients like blood oranges and apricots that grow bountifully in Europe but struggle on our shores. It's the ingredients grown in heated greenhouses in the midst of winter or flown across the world that are out of bounds for me. Buying produce with thousands of air miles behind it feels like madness when the natural world is in crisis. Look at the labels in your shops to find out what is reasonably local and be as sustainably-minded as you can.

Seasoning

When I trained at the restaurant, our head chef, Paul, would stand at the pass, tasting and plating everything that went to the tables. Every single thing I cooked, whether it was a pan of lentils, some Swiss chard, romesco or aïoli, would first go to him to try before it went to anyone else. On the good days, he would kindly encourage a touch more mustard in the lentils, more lemon on the Swiss chard or salt in the aïoli. On the bad ones, I would be chastised for not grinding up my pinches of sea salt finely enough, not caramelising the pumpkins adequately or forgetting that crucial touch of lemon juice on the burrata. And through his constant assessment, critique and encouragement I learnt what seasoning really means.

In the recipes that follow you'll often see the phrase, 'taste and adjust the seasoning as necessary'. But I wanted to explain what that really means. Seasoning is the art of bringing the best out of the ingredients in your dish, so that it bursts with flavour. It is about finding balance and harmony, and generally revolves around salt, fat and acid. Cooking without tasting is like painting blindfolded and expecting to produce a masterpiece. Watch a great chef at work and they cannot help but taste as they go, dipping fingers and spoons, constantly adjusting and taking part in the entire journey of the dish, whether it be marmalade, cake batter or a slow-cooked stew. So many of us cooks at home will technically follow a recipe to the letter, but make the crucial mistake of not tasting or seasoning right until the end.

Salt works to enhance flavour by heightening natural sugars and aromas while suppressing excessive bitterness. Take a spear of purple sprouting broccoli, boil it in water and eat it. As I explained above, the better an ingredient, the better the starting point. If it's a well-grown spear of broccoli, you're off to a good start. But add some salt to the water while the broccoli is cooking, enough that you can actually taste a slight saltiness (a teeny pinch is utterly pointless), and your broccoli will come to life. There is a great difference in having salt on top of your food at the end and salting your food as you cook. You want the salt to be inside what you're eating for maximum flavour, and a big pinch of salt at the end is only going to make the dish salty, not enhance the flavour.

Salt is also an ingredient in itself, and the quality of salt you use will have a drastic effect on the final flavour of the dish. I use flaky sea salt for my main seasoning, but would never waste such good salt in a pot of pasta water for instance – for that I use a decent, but cheaper, grey or rock salt. Also, by always using the same salt, I find my fingers have learnt the weight of the pinch I need to add. Because seasoning is a muscle that you need to train, it takes practice. If you always use the same tools, it well help build that instinct. Often if I'm away and use a salt that I'm not used to, I can find myself over-seasoning a dish.

The final thing to understand about salt is that it not only helps with flavour, but also plays a crucial part in the cooking process. Fry courgettes or onions in olive oil without salt and they burn easily and take longer to cook. Whereas adding a decent pinch of salt as you cook them not only enhances flavour, but also draws out moisture and helps them to break down so they cook in their own concentrated juices. Season a steak liberally and leave the salt to work its way into the meat before you start cooking, which will not only help tenderise, but also hold on to moisture from within as the meat cooks, resulting in a juicier and more flavourful steak.

Fat is another essential part of seasoning and is a carrier for flavour, helping to round out a dish. It also helps with the absorption of key vitamins and minerals. Imagine it as an enabler that comes in many different forms: olive oil, burrata, yoghurt, butter, pancetta, lard and guanciale. You've also got crème fraîche, coconut milk, rapeseed oil and ghee. Fat creates mouthfeel and unctuousness while also being incredibly helpful in certain cooking processes, allowing flavours to come together and keeping things juicy.

Lastly, you have acidity, which is so important in tandem with salt to help brighten and round out flavour. It cuts through fat, providing a vital foil to the richness while also having great flavour itself, which can be very complementary when cooking. But acids are strong and need to be used carefully, as it's very easy to overwhelm a dish. Think of a bolognese, which uses the gentle acidity of tomato to brighten the rich fatty ragù – a squeeze of lemon on top would utterly overwhelm that subtle marriage of flavour. Whereas a squeeze of lemon on a buttery head of broccoli or fillet of fish is sheer joy. Think of fat and acidity as the yin and yang of cooking, and salt as the constant to bring out flavour. You do not always need to use all three. A carbonara is a great example, where you have a few different fats and salts working together to create a rich silky sauce that doesn't need acidity anywhere near it.

Seasoning is an incredibly complex world to explain, but practice makes perfect and I think it is something you can quite easily learn. The key is to use your instincts, tasting constantly, and making small adjustments, little and often. And as I said earlier, while seasoning is absolutely key, it can only enhance flavour. If you combine careful seasoning with seasonal produce, you will transform the quality of your cooking.

To me the act of cooking is creative, playful and instinctual. Even if I cook the same dish twice, it's rare for it to turn out exactly the same each time. Cooking is about adapting to what you have in front of you. So, while I have tested and tested these recipes, honing them to give you the best chance of replicating them, it is important to remember that ingredients vary, your pans are different, as is your olive oil, your oven, your pinch of salt and, most importantly, your tastebuds! Use these recipes as a guide, but I urge you not to follow them blindly. You need to cook with your senses and intuition. Knowing that so much variability exists when writing and following a recipe, there are a few things I wanted to mention:

FIRST, to avoid mistakes it helps to read a recipe through before you start cooking. Ensure you understand the steps before you begin.

OLIVE OIL. I have never and will never use a tablespoon to measure olive oil. I pour it into my pan or over my dish with joyful abundance, instinctively looking for the right amount to help whatever it is I'm cooking. In this book, however, I have given a rough guide in places that I thought you might need it, other times I've left it up to you. Please only take these as a guide, if you feel your dish needs a glug more, go ahead! Secondly, I always buy my olive oil in large 5-litre tins, which means I get quality oil at a fair price, I recommend you do the same. Odysea is a particular favourite.

CHILLI. I love chilli and use a lot of it. The key with chilli in this kind of cooking is that you are adding flavour first with gentle heat second. Please don't overwhelm your dish with an overgenerous handful of taste-numbing fire. Know your chilli flakes well, add them little by little to get the balance right for you, and be careful when cooking, they burn easily.

PRODUCE. As with chilli, produce varies greatly in flavour and strength depending on the quality, the variety and the season in which it was grown. The same weight of ginger can vary massively in strength, as can the acidity of lemons and the heat of garlic etc. Remember we are cooking with different ingredients, so you need to adapt to what you have in front of you. Don't go squeezing over a whole half of lemon because I said so and end up finding your dish too lemony. Add little by little and get the balance right for your palate.

OVENS VARY GREATLY. You have hot spots, cold spots, your temperature gauge may be slightly off, your oven bigger or smaller and therefore your cake closer to the hot roof or fan. You know your oven better than I do, so if you see your cake browning or your meat burning just turn the temperature down slightly. Adapt to your oven and keep an eye no matter what time I've instructed. Just be careful when baking not to open the oven door too early.

MEAT. Your chicken might be bigger or smaller, your lamb fattier, your steak thicker, your pan thinner or your heat hotter. It is so hard to give exact times for cooking meat or fish because there is so much variability. The key is to learn what you're looking for. Meat probes are a very helpful tool, and I recommend you get one. But also use your instincts, you can always take something out of the oven early and have a test. Give your meat time to rest for it to reabsorb its juices and remember that it will continue to cook when out of the oven. The ideal is to take your meat out just before it is ready and allow the resting time for it to finish cooking. If you can achieve this, you will be eating very well indeed.

ONIONS. I generally always use decent size brown onions, if you only have those small ones, use two to my one in the recipe.

BEANS. While tins are brilliant and cheap as chips, I prefer using jarred beans, which are softer and have a superior flavour. Tinned beans are often much harder. So, if using tins, use two per one large jar, pour them into a pan, season with a pinch of salt and pour in just enough water so that they're completely submerged. Simmer with the lid on for about 15-20 minutes until you can squish a bean between two fingers.

HERBS. I use them by the handful and in great abundance. They're my favourite thing to grow at home and I highly recommend you plant some in your garden or on your windowsill. Particularly the hardy varieties as, once established, they come back year after year.

Lastly, but perhaps most important of all. I have designed these recipes for my tastes. These are the dishes I love and cook often, I hope they become staples for you at home too. But please play with them and adapt them to your liking. Work with the seasons and use the ideas that follow throughout the year by varying the produce according to what you have around you. Recipes are not rules to be followed, they are guides to be enjoyed.

WINTER

WINTER IS THE PRICE YOU PAY FOR LIVING IN THE COUNTRYSIDE. It is a starkly beautiful season, mother nature laid bare for all to see. Still and peaceful, yet wild and ruthless. Sharp heavy frosts blanket the land in a quiet fog broken only by the bones of trees. Unrelenting rain and impenetrable clouds steal the sun for weeks. We work outside, battling penetrating wind with rosy cheeks, dragon breath and fingers so stiff with cold they hurt. Dorset mizzle refuses to rain but leaves you soaked, and the long, quiet nights come with iron skies and haunting moons. It is a time for self-reflection, crackling fires and hearty cooking. A time for slowing down and taking stock. Recharging, uncoiling and preparing for the bustle of spring.

Sometimes, after weeks yearning for the warm green of spring through the bitter cold, I wake to a stillness that only exists in winter. There is a mere whisper of wind, the air so clean and crisp it fizzes in my nostrils; shafts of sun cast the bare trees into shadowed silhouettes of gilded silver light. The birds always seem to save their song for days like these, clearing the cobwebs from their throats and heralding the returning sun after weeks quietly sheltering from the cold. There is such a pure beauty to days like these, nature unadorned and laid bare, all the sweeter after weeks of cruel unforgiving weather.

Crystalline grass crunches pleasingly underfoot, jewelled cobwebs hang with dew like a necklace of pearls and the hopeful buds of spring begin to appear in the hedgerows. Clouds of frogspawn shimmer on the edge of the pond, the frogs' mating calls a rhythmic chorus of croaks among the garrulous chatter of our resident ducks. Newts begin to appear in cracks and crevices all over the house, creeping their way out from hibernation with the impending warmth of spring. I gather them up when I find them, their bodies slow and cold in my hand after months of stillness, taking them back towards the damp parts of the garden so they too can begin the rituals of spring.

Winter work is tough, monotonous and challenging. It's when the animals need me most, and I spend my days tied to the farm, topping up hay racks, chipping ice from water troughs and trimming damp, muddy hooves. I carry hay from field to field, the bales heavy on my shoulder as scratchy grasses catch in my woolly jumper and creep down my neck. Tearing open the bales, I breathe deeply, enjoying the nostalgic scent of dried summer grasses, and watch the dust hovering in sharp beams of light. You can tell good hay from the smell and the colour within. Ours is hot and fragrant, much of the grass still a gentle emerald green and full of dried wildflowers and their seedheads: vetch pods, sharp thistles, yellow rattle pods and spears of knapweed and ox-eye. The goats jostle around me, jumping on the hay as I fluff it into the rack, crunching happily on great wads of dried grass and butting each other for pole position. I love the sound of their teeth grinding away and always take the time to sit with them for a while, watching closely, scratching their chins and looking for the first signs of a limp, which is common in these winter months as the damp ground wreaks havoc on their hooves. In late winter, if you watch closely, you can often catch the kicking hoof of a yet to be born kid goat pressing through the nannies' bulging bellies. I'll begin to guess at who's carrying twins and who a singleton and give those with twins extra rations ahead of birthing in spring.

My patient sheep sit high on the hill, uninterested in the hay I offer them, eyes closed and breathing deeply. They warm their backs in the sun, legs tucked underneath a shaggy cocoon of wool. Soon we'll be lambing, and this quiet peace will be broken by the cheerful bleats of gambolling lambs chasing each other round the field as kid goats climb their mothers. Unlike the nannies, who loudly display all signs of pregnancy in their waddle and melodramatic discomfort, the sheep are very private and stoic, hiding any signs of distress behind dark eyes and a thick coat of wool. I sit and watch them each day, looking for swelling udders or particularly wide ewes with obvious twins. But mostly I just let them get used to me ahead of the imminent chaos, so that when I step in to help with a tricky birth it isn't cause for them to worry.

Sometimes from my perch I'll see our resident fox emerging from the goyle in which she lives. Creeping her way through the tangled meadow below, stalking silently, low to the ground with ears pricked high. With a sudden pounce she leaps into a tuft of grass and emerges with a fat juicy vole, purposefully hiding it in the grass while continuing to hunt, catching a few more and placing them in the ever-growing pile. When the area is depleted, she goes back to the pile and carries it to a new patch to continue the hunt. Crows hover high above, hoping to steal from the unprotected stash. But Mrs Fox is cunning and never strays too far, running back if need be to ward off swooping crows. After three movements of the growing pile, I watch her gather the voles in a huge mouthful, the tails dangling from her teeth as she secretes them back to her den in the woods. I hope I get a glimpse of the cubs in spring.

Inside, the fire is always crackling and the windows shimmer with mist. Boots live by the warmth of the stove, socks hang from the rail above and bums press against oven doors while we chat away in the peaceful kitchen. The slowness of winter lends itself to long days of careful cooking and it's rare that a broth doesn't simmer on the stove, or a stew gently blip away in a low oven. I love the comforting warmth of winter food, studded by the dark iron green of kales and cabbages that sweeten in the frost. We bring in armfuls of blue silvery leeks, washing them in the sink and chopping them roughly with torn handfuls of cavolo nero for dark green soups spiked with chorizo and finished with lashings of olive oil. Tough cuts of meat tenderly cook for hours until unctuous and giving, before being piled on to beds of buttery mash. Winter might be a leaner period when cooking seasonally, but I think the food in this chapter is perhaps my favourite of all. This is a time for soulful feel-good cooking, where nourishment and warmth are the main objectives, and I hope the food to come feeds you in more ways than one.

CRAB TOAST
with fennel & blood orange

LIVING ON THE DORSET COAST, WE ARE LUCKY TO HAVE ACCESS to some really special fresh crab. Crab is very sustainable – there are a lot of them around our coast, and we catch more than the rest of Europe, exporting far more than we eat. Most importantly, though, our method of catching them in pots is very selective. Undersized and female crabs are put straight back, and there's not really any by-catch, especially when compared to the unbelievably destructive methods of dredging and trawling. One of our local farm shops sells them ready to go, cooked and picked in the shell, a real treat to take home since all the hard work is already done. In spring I love using crab in a risotto (see page 126), in summer with linguine, but in winter we make the most of the citrus season and serve it on buttery toast, with lots of lemon and parsley and this fresh, zingy salad of raw fennel and blood orange. It's really simple to make and beautiful to eat.

SERVES 2 AS A MAIN,
OR 4 AS A STARTER

1 picked crab (both white and brown meat)

2 tbsp mayo, homemade (see page 307), or quality shop-bought

1 lemon

a bunch of fresh parsley

2 blood oranges

1 bulb of fennel

1 head of radicchio or treviso

olive oil

a bunch of fresh parsley or tarragon

hot buttered toast, for serving

Put the brown crabmeat into a bowl with the mayo, then squeeze in a dash of lemon juice (start with about a third of the lemon) and mix well. The brown meat should almost melt into the mayo and form a beautiful sauce. Finely chop the parsley and add to the bowl with the white crabmeat, a pinch of salt and lots of pepper, and gently stir through. Have a taste and check your seasoning – it should be delicious, but may need a squeak more lemon and some salt.

Using a sharp knife, peel the oranges, then cut into segments with no pith: you do this by just following the white lines to cut out the lovely segments of flesh – it's such a satisfying process. Put them in a bowl with any juice that has collected on your chopping board, then finely shave in the fennel. Tear in the radicchio, then drizzle over some quality olive oil and add a squeeze of lemon, salt and pepper. Give it all a good stir and chuck in the finely chopped parsley. Spread the crab thickly on hot buttered toast and serve with the salad and a wedge of lemon. Enjoy!

PISSALADIÈRE

I THINK THIS IS ONE OF THE MOST USEFUL RECIPES to have in your arsenal and, though it's quite well known, it's not made by home cooks as often as it should be. It's so simple to make, particularly if you use shop-bought puff pastry as I always do. The joy of a pissaladière is the contrast between a wonderfully sweet base of onion and the salty anchovy and olive above. There is no trick to it really, just the time and patience needed to really cook down those onions until they're sweet and tender. Usually I make this as a bite to serve with drinks before dinner and it always goes down a storm, but it also makes a sprightly lunch alongside a simple salad.

SERVES 10 AS AN
APPETISER, OR 4–6
AS A LIGHT LUNCH

10 large brown onions

50g butter

3 tbsp olive oil

*1 sheet of ready-made
all-butter puff pastry*

3 tins of anchovies

*1 jar of pitted Kalamata
olives, 160g drained
weight*

1 egg

*a handful of fresh thyme
leaves*

Slice the onions thinly. Chuck the butter and olive oil into a large heavy-based pan and, once the butter is melted, add the onions with a splash of water and a generous pinch of salt. Cook on a medium heat for about 30 minutes, until they are wonderfully sweet and tender – but be incredibly careful that they don't burn and catch on the bottom of the pan. When ready, turn off the heat and leave to cool (I often do this the night before).

Preheat your oven to 200°C fan.

Roll out the pastry on a sheet of baking parchment and place on a baking tray. Two fingers' width from the edge, score a line with a sharp knife to create a frame around the pastry, not cutting all the way through. This line allows the outer layers of puff pastry to rise above the filling and form a lovely crust. Spread the onions over the inside of the frame, right to the edge of your lines but not going over. Place the anchovies on top of the onions in diagonal lines, creating a diamond trellis. Rinse the olives, shake dry and dot one in the centre of each diamond. Whisk the egg and brush the edge of the pastry, then place in the oven for about 30 minutes, until the pastry has puffed at the edges and gone a lovely golden brown.

Remove from the oven, sprinkle with the thyme and serve while still warm.

BAKED VACHERIN
with Swiss chard & pink fir apple potatoes

A BAKED VACHERIN TENDS TO GET RELEGATED TO THE END OF THE MEAL as an exciting part of a cheeseboard. But I like putting it centre stage, as a main or starter to be shared with lots of lovely things to dip and dunk in the funky molten cheese. New potatoes are a must – I love the sweet crunch of pink fir apple for this, but any potato works well. Swiss chard is incredible with Vacherin, the minerally earthiness just perfect against the cheese. Bread is key, as are cornichons; a little cured ham is great, but not essential, and a mustardy green chicory salad is excellent.

SERVES 2 GENEROUSLY
AS A MAIN, OR 4 AS A
STARTER

1 Vacherin Mont d'Or,
 in its box
500g pink fir apple or
 similar potatoes
50g butter
a bunch of fresh chives
400g Swiss chard
olive oil
juice of ½ lemon
1 baguette
a handful of cornichons
cured ham (optional)
1 head of frisée lettuce, and
 some radicchio or chicory

Preheat your oven to 160°C fan.

Remove any packaging from the Vacherin, inside and out, then place it back in its box. Poke a few holes in the top of the cheese – some like to bury a few sprigs of thyme or shards of garlic in the holes. Put the lid on the box and place in the oven for about 30 minutes – the test is that, when giving it a jiggle, the middle should be clearly molten. While the Vacherin is in the oven, chuck the potatoes in a pan, top up with warm water, season well and bring up to a simmer. Cook until tender when skewered with a knife. Strain, return to the pan, add a generous knob of butter, the finely chopped chives, and season generously with salt and pepper. Roughly halve any larger potatoes and mix well to coat in the butter. Leave in the pot with the lid on, to keep warm.

While the spuds are cooking, get the Swiss chard going. Strip the leaves from the stalks and cut the stalks into finger-length pieces. Bring a pan of seasoned water to the boil and plunge in the stalks, cook for about 3–5 minutes, until tender, then add the leaves and cook for another minute or so. Strain, making sure to get out all the water, drizzle generously with olive oil, and season with some salt and a squeeze of lemon.

Warm the bread in the oven and tear or cut into chunks. Bring out the Vacherin and place in the centre of a tray or large plate. Surround with the potatoes, chard, baguette, cornichons, cured ham, if using, and salad. Then scoop, dip and dunk to your heart's content.

ROAST PUMPKIN, BUFFALO MOZZARELLA, SAGE & HAZELNUTS

THIS FORMAT OF BEAUTIFULLY COOKED SEASONAL VEG, on a bed of cheese, with herbs and toasted nuts, is a very useful thing to know. At Noble Rot, the restaurant where I learnt so much, a version of this dish was always on the menu, whether it be with Roscoff onions in autumn, calçots and romesco in spring, or the mighty Crown Prince pumpkin in winter. The key, of course, is that when cooking something so simple you need to start with quality ingredients, sourced locally and grown with love in the season in which they were meant to be grown. Here the pumpkin is roasted until the sugars begin to caramelise, the toasted nuts exaggerate and complement the nuttiness of the pumpkin, the zing of lemon brings it to life, and the sage brings it back to earth.

SERVES 4

1 pumpkin (Crown Prince
  is a favourite variety)
6 tbsp olive oil
50g blanched hazelnuts
12 fresh sage leaves
250g buffalo mozzarella
1 unwaxed lemon

Preheat your oven to 200°C fan and line a baking tray with baking parchment. Scrub the pumpkin and cut it into wedges. Toss the wedges with 3 tablespoons of olive oil, season with salt, then spread on the baking tray and roast for 30–40 minutes, until caramelised and tender. When ready, remove from the oven and scrape off the pumpkin seeds. (I find this much easier to do once the wedges are cooked.)

While the pumpkin roasts, add the hazelnuts to a small ovenproof pan and toast in the oven for 10 minutes until golden and crisp, then transfer to a pestle and mortar and lightly crush. Place the pan on a medium heat and add 3 tablespoons of olive oil. Once shimmering, add the sage leaves and fry for 30–60 seconds, until just crisp, then transfer to a plate lined with kitchen paper.

To serve, tear some mozzarella on to each plate and top with a couple of pumpkin wedges. Finish with a generous drizzle of olive oil, the hazelnuts, sage leaves, a little lemon zest and a squeeze of the juice.

SPICED CHICKEN LIVER *&* GRILLED SHALLOT
BRUSCHETTA WITH CHIVES

I SEE CHICKEN LIVER AS THE GATEWAY INTO THE WORLD OF OFFAL. It's sweet, rich and meltingly tender. Personally, I can't get enough of the stuff, but it wasn't always that way. My granny was Dutch, and food was part of her soul. The kitchen was her studio and she was an artist. If I close my eyes, I can smell her spice cabinet and picture the jar of homemade elderflower cordial in her fridge, the lid so sticky it was almost locked to us kids. I miss her curried marrow soup and spicy chicken wings, the cinnamon toasts we'd bake in the Aga to have with hot cocoa, and her glinting eyes and knowing smile. She used to delight in watching us squirm in front of cumin-spiced livers, ox-tongue and devilled kidneys, not allowed to leave the table until our plates were clean. I learnt to just wolf them down while still warm, but my stubborn brothers made the mistake of letting them grow cold and they'd sit there for hours while she did the crossword. I'm glad of it, though, as I am now a fanatical lover of liver in all forms. So this dish is a homage to her, and to the skills and attitudes towards food that she passed down to Mum, and then on to me.

SERVES 4

8 round shallots (not the tiny pickling ones)

2 tbsp olive oil

400g chicken livers

a generous pinch of ground allspice

a careful pinch of ground cloves

½ nutmeg

3 cloves of garlic

a few sprigs of fresh rosemary

40g butter

a generous splash of brandy or Madeira

100ml double cream

for serving

4 slices of good bread (ciabatta or sourdough), for toasting

a small bunch of fresh chives

Preheat your oven to 220°C on the fan-grill setting.

Peel and halve the shallots, then place in a single layer on a small baking tray and drizzle with the olive oil. Season well and place in the oven for about 30–40 minutes, until they are caramelised and tender – a little char here and there is great, just don't incinerate them. Remove from the oven and leave to cool.

Rinse the livers, pat dry and trim away any sinew, then roughly chop into bite-size pieces. Place in a bowl, add the spices, grate in the nutmeg, season well with salt and pepper and mix thoroughly. Finely slice the garlic and finely chop the rosemary.

The shallots should be cool enough to handle by now; separate them into individual petals and taste to check the seasoning; adjust with a touch more salt if necessary. Get your toast on, and put a wide frying pan on a medium heat. Chuck in the butter and add the garlic and rosemary. Let this sizzle briefly, but before the garlic browns, add the livers and whack the heat to max. Fry on each side for just a minute, trying to get some good caramelisation/colour, while keeping the liver blushing pink within. Chuck in the shallots,

pour in the brandy and toss together. Let the brandy
evaporate for a few seconds, then pour in the cream and stir
through. Butter the toast, spoon the livers generously on top,
finish with finely chopped chives and tuck in immediately.
Note that this is equally good in a muffin, on creamy polenta,
in pasta or even blitzed into a coarse pâté.

PUY LENTILS
with spinach & pancetta

I LOVE PUY LENTILS – THEY'RE HEALTHY, PACKED WITH PROTEIN and an amazing base for all sorts of flavours. I find they're particularly good with quality sausages and a mustardy aïoli, but equally so with pan-fried fish and salsa verde, or slow-roast lamb and anchovy. Here they're pictured with pumpkin roasted in a hot oven until sweet and charred, and finished with goat's cheese. It's a great combo, but this recipe is really all about the lentils. Any leftovers make a great pasta sauce when finished with a drizzle of chilli oil and parmesan, or you can water them down a bit, add some curry powder and turn them into curried lentil soup, an old favourite of my granny's.

SERVES 6

1 large brown onion

1 leek

2 carrots

3 celery sticks

4 tbsp olive oil

150g diced pancetta (optional)

a generous glass of white wine

500g Puy lentils

5 bay leaves

a few sprigs of fresh thyme

1 litre chicken stock (see page 306), veg stock or water

500g spinach

1 heaped tbsp Dijon mustard

a big handful of fresh parsley

Finely dice the onion, leek, carrots and celery. Heat the olive oil in a large pan, then add the veg and the pancetta, if using. Season well and cook gently for 15–20 minutes, until soft and sweet.

Add the wine and cook off the alcohol, then rinse the lentils in a sieve and add to the pan, giving them a good stir. Follow with the bay leaves, thyme and stock, adding just enough to barely cover the lentils. Bring to a gentle simmer and cook for around 30 minutes, until the lentils are tender and beginning to open but still have a nice bit of bite to them. When ready, add the spinach and cook until barely wilted, then take off the heat, add the mustard and the finely chopped parsley. Give it a good stir and taste to check your seasoning – it'll need a hefty pinch of salt and pepper, and often some more mustard, so adjust as necessary. This keeps in the fridge for a good few days – just make sure to reheat it properly.

SARDINE PUTTANESCA

PUTTANESCA IS THE ULTIMATE STORE CUPBOARD DISH . . . everything comes from a jar or a tin, and it's one of my all-time favourites, a perfect marriage of richness, acidity and salinity that packs a punch and explodes with flavour. There's chilli, handfuls of garlic and deep undertones of anchovy. But this version has the added bonus of tinned sardines, turning it into a properly hearty meal that can be rustled up in no time without having to head for the shops. Rich with flavour and simple to execute, expect bowls licked clean and the pot scraped bare.

SERVES 5

1 large red onion

olive oil

5 cloves of garlic

1 tsp chilli flakes

8 anchovies

1 tbsp tomato purée

2 x 400g tins of plum tomatoes

80g capers

140g pitted Kalamata olives

30g butter

½ tbsp sugar

2 tins of quality sardines

500g pasta

a bunch of fresh parsley

Finely dice the onion and fry in a heavy-based pan with lots of olive oil and a generous pinch of salt until sweet and tender. When ready, finely chop the garlic and add to the onion along with the chilli flakes and the anchovies. Cook gently for a few minutes, smushing the anchovies with a wooden spoon until they melt and infuse into the oil. Then add the tomato purée and cook out for a minute before pouring in the tinned tomatoes. Rinse the tins with a splash of water and add half a tin of this tomatoey water to the pan. Simmer for 20 minutes, stirring occasionally until the sauce has thickened.

At this point, drain the capers and olives and rinse under a tap. Shake dry, then add to the sauce with the butter. Mix well and continue cooking for a few minutes so they become one with the sauce; taste to check your seasoning, only adding salt carefully as many of the ingredients are quite salty. Add the sugar to balance out the acidity. Drain off the sardines, then add to the pan and gently break them apart – I don't like to smash them up too much. Turn the heat off and crack on with the pasta.

Make sure to properly season your pasta water and cook the pasta until al dente. Bring the sauce back up to heat just before it's done. Reserve a mugful of the pasta cooking water before you strain it off. Add this little by little as you whip the sauce into the pasta. Finish with the finely chopped parsley, mix again and serve with a drizzle of really good olive oil.

DEEP GREEN PASTA

IN WINTER I CRAVE BIG REVITALISING POPEYE HITS OF GREEN. This recipe is delicious, made in one pot, takes 15 minutes and just so happens to be vegan . . . need I say more. I particularly love this sauce stirred through pasta, BUT it's equally delicious dolloped into a risotto in its final stages, stirred through white beans, slathered on toast with eggs, even stirred into a salad dressing. It's bracingly simple and wonderfully nourishing.

SERVES 4

250g cavolo nero

2–3 cloves of garlic, peeled

200g spinach

400g rigatoni

100ml olive oil

1 unwaxed lemon

*ricotta, parmesan or
    pecorino, for serving
    (optional)*

Get a large pan of water on to a rolling boil and season well with salt, enough that you can actually taste it. Add the cavolo nero along with the garlic cloves and simmer for about 5 minutes. Then add the spinach, and when it has wilted, which won't take long at all, keeping the pot of water at a rolling boil, lift the greens and garlic into a colander. Run the greens under a cold tap and allow to drain. Chuck the pasta into the pan of water.

When the greens are drained, transfer to a high-speed blender (a Nutribullet/Vitamix is ideal for this), pour in the olive oil, grate in the zest of the lemon and blitz into a very smooth purée, adding a splash of the cooking water to loosen it if need be. Taste and adjust the seasoning as necessary.

Cook the pasta until al dente, then take a mug and collect a full cup of the starchy water before straining the pasta. Pour the pasta back into the hot pan and add a few big dollops of the sauce – be generous. Add a good splash of the pasta water and really mix well, beating it around the pan to form a thick sauce that envelops the pasta in a deep green blanket. Serve immediately, with a squeeze of lemon, some ricotta, parmesan or pecorino, if you like, and a generous drizzle of olive oil.

PASTA E CECI

THE FIRST TIME I TRIED PASTA E CECI, I FELL UTTERLY IN LOVE and couldn't stop making it for months. The flavour and texture are supremely comforting and, at the risk of offending our Italian cousins, I liken its soothing qualities to a grown-up beans on toast. Depending on where you are in Italy, pasta e ceci changes drastically from region to region. In the poorer south, it appears in its purest form, made with eggless semolina pasta, chickpeas and maybe a little tomato. Whereas, as you move north into the wealthier and more abundant regions, anchovies begin to appear in the soffritto base, with rich egg pasta and generous chunks of pancetta. I love it in all these forms, particularly with good pancetta, and depending on the weather, who's around and what's in the fridge, I often throw in some of these luxurious extras. But for this book I thought I'd show you just how good it can be in its humblest form. My only request is that you use one of those quality jars of cooked chickpeas.

SERVES 4

3 cloves of garlic

1 brown onion

1 leek

1 carrot

4 tbsp olive oil

a pinch of chilli flakes

2 sprigs of fresh rosemary

3 bay leaves

1 tbsp tomato purée

1 x 400g tin of plum
   tomatoes

1 x 700g jar of quality
   chickpeas

350g small soup-type pasta
   (ditali, macaroni etc.)

Finely dice the garlic, onion, leek and carrot. Pour the oil into a wide heavy-based pan, add the garlic, chilli flakes, whole rosemary sprigs and bay, and turn the heat on. This allows the garlic, etc. to slowly infuse the oil without burning while the pan heats up. After a few minutes, the garlic will be sizzling. Before it begins to colour, add the onion, leek and carrot with a generous pinch of salt. Cook right down until sweet and tender, about 10 minutes, then add the tomato purée. Mix this through and cook out the purée for a few minutes.

Using scissors, chop the tomatoes inside the tin to break them up as best you can. I prefer to use plum tomatoes, not chopped, because their flavour is so much better. Pour these into the pan, then rinse out the tin with a splash of water and pour that tomatoey water into the pan too. Bring to a gentle simmer, pour in half the chickpeas and cook for 15 minutes so the flavours can get to know each other. Pour the other half into a pestle and mortar or food processor and mash into a paste, then add to the pan.

Cook your pasta until it's a few minutes off ready, then add to the pan with a splash of the starchy water to finish cooking. Taste and adjust the seasoning as needed. Spoon into bowls and finish with a drizzle of olive oil.

CABBAGE, BACON & POTATO SOUP

A ROBUST BOWL OF STEAMING BROTH WITH SMOKY BACON, curly leaves of deep green cabbage and yielding potatoes on the brink of collapse. This hearty peasant dish is older than time itself. When the winter weather sets in, with boots caked in mud, fingers stiff with cold and cheeks flushed from icy winds, this is the kind of food you want to come home to. All you need is a stout drink and a hunk of crusty bread and this will warm you to the core. With food this simple, the quality of your ingredients is key – I recommend making your own broth, buying a stunning cabbage and some damn good bacon.

SERVES 4

250g smoked streaky bacon
olive oil
4 cloves of garlic
3–5 sprigs of fresh thyme
2 large brown onions
2 baking potatoes
a glass of white wine
*1.2 litres really good chicken
  stock (see page 306)*
1 Savoy cabbage
*a large handful of fresh
  parsley*
⅔ nutmeg
*bread and butter,
  for serving*

Remove the rind from the bacon, cut into jaunty chunks, place in a wide heavy-based pan, drizzle in some olive oil and turn the heat to medium. Very finely slice the garlic and add to the bacon along with the thyme sprigs. You want to gently and slowly cook this down, not looking for any colour or caramelisation, just rendering the fat out of the bacon and infusing it with the garlic and thyme. While this is frying, finely slice the onions and add to the pan. Season generously with salt and cook the onions until they are sweet and tender, about 10–15 minutes. While the onions are cooking, peel the potatoes and cut into large chunks. When the onions are beginning to colour, pour in the white wine and use your wooden spoon to scrape the bottom of the pan and unstick any caramelisation. When the wine has evaporated, add the potatoes and pour in the stock.

Some cabbages can be huge and some can be small, so it's difficult for me to give you a precise amount. But just start pulling off the leaves, tearing them into large chunks and adding to the pan. You want quite a lot, more than the potato, as this is the body of the soup. Season again, then put the lid on and bring up to a simmer. When the cabbage has relaxed into the broth, remove the lid and let it gently simmer with the potatoes until both are well cooked. Finely chop the parsley and add to the pan, grate in the nutmeg, then stir and taste. Adjust the seasoning as necessary, and serve in deep bowls with lavishly buttered bread.

COMTÉ CHEESE & ONION TART

I HAVE SUCH FOND MEMORIES OF DRIVING THROUGH FRANCE as a young boy, the car loaded to the ceiling with our bags, legs tangled in the back and fighting for space with the dogs. Every now and then we'd stop in a little village and grab something to eat from the local boulangerie or restaurant, and depending what was on offer we'd be eating various quiches, buttery croissants or ham and baguettes. But of these offerings, it was always the cheese and onion tarts that stole the show for me, sometimes with bacon, often without, the custard just holding together a mess of slow-cooked onions. This makes a particularly fine and hearty winter lunch with a mustardy green salad.

SERVES 6–8

shortcrust pastry (see recipe on page 309) or 1 sheet shop-bought

1 egg, beaten

for the filling

5 large brown onions

50g butter

a small glass of white wine

a few sprigs of fresh thyme

120g Comté cheese

150ml whole milk

150ml double cream

3 eggs

Thinly slice the onions, add to the pan with the butter and season well with salt. Put the lid on and cook slowly for about 30 minutes, stirring often, until sweet and wonderfully tender – a little bit of caramelisation is OK, but be careful they don't burn. When the onions are cooked, deglaze the pan with the wine, cook off the liquid, then turn off the heat.

Preheat your oven to 170°C fan.

On a lightly floured surface, roll out the pastry to about 3mm thick. Lift into a 25cm tart tin with a removeable base, then take a little piece of dough from the edge and use this to gently press the pastry into the tin, leaving an overhang around the sides. Prick the pastry base all over with a fork and chill in the freezer for 20 minutes. Then line the pastry with baking parchment and fill with baking beans. Put the tin on to a baking tray and bake for 15–20 minutes, until the pastry is firm, then remove the beans and parchment, brush with egg and return to the oven for another 10 minutes, until golden. Trim off any excess pastry with a serrated knife.

Pick the thyme leaves. Coarsely grate the Comté and set aside 20g. Put the other 100g into a bowl with the milk, cream, eggs and thyme, then thoroughly mix together. Season well with salt and pepper, then pour in the onions and mix again. Pour 80% of the mixture into the blind-baked pastry case, making sure the onion is evenly dispersed before placing the tray in the oven. Once the tray is in the oven,

carefully pour in the rest of the mixture, making sure none of it seeps down the sides of the pastry. Sprinkle with the reserved cheese and bake for about 30 minutes, until the top begins to caramelise and the centre of the tart is set (check by giving the tray a gentle jiggle). Leave to cool for 15 minutes, then carefully remove from the case, slice and serve with a sharp green salad.

PUMPKIN, SPINACH & MOZZARELLA LASAGNE

THIS IS A RICH AND WARMING ROAST PUMPKIN LASAGNE, layered with a spinach béchamel and torn mozzarella. It has a beautiful contrast between the vibrant orange and dark green, with sweet earthy flavours and a minerally oomph. There are little squeaks of nutmeg and lemon zest, which add a lovely zing, and I often make it with goat's cheese instead, for that salty funk that goes so well with pumpkin. A traditional lasagne is quite a lengthy thing to make, but compared to the classic, which needs both a bolognese and a béchamel, this is pretty easy and well worth the effort.

SERVES 6

1 pumpkin
6 tbsp olive oil
3 cloves of garlic
800g spinach
1 unwaxed lemon
500g fresh lasagne sheets
400g mozzarella
a little parmesan

for the béchamel
70g butter
70g plain flour
1 litre whole milk
2 bay leaves
½ nutmeg

Preheat your oven to 200°C fan.

Peel the pumpkin, cut in half and remove the seeds. Chop into roughly 1cm cubes, then spread out over a large baking tray about 35cm x 25cm. Drizzle with 4 tablespoons of olive oil, season and mix well. Roast for 20–25 minutes, until tender and lightly caramelised. While the pumpkin is roasting, finely slice the garlic and gently fry in 2 tablespoons of olive oil on a low heat in a large pan. Before the garlic takes on any colour, add the spinach (you'll probably need to do this in batches), season well and let it briefly wilt down. Transfer to a blender or food processor but don't blitz yet, leave it to cool while you make the béchamel.

Melt the butter in a pan on a low heat, then add the flour and whisk for a few minutes. It should thicken and go biscuity brown. Pour in the milk little by little, stirring continuously to prevent lumps. Add the bay leaves and grate in the nutmeg. Keep stirring until the milk thickens to a lovely sauce that coats the back of a spoon, season well and take off the heat.

Add the spinach to the béchamel and blitz with the zest of a lemon and a dash of lemon juice until completely smooth. Taste to check the seasoning.

Bring a wide pan of water to a rolling boil and season well with salt. Working in batches, blanch the lasagne sheets for 1–2 minutes, then transfer to cold water to stop them

CONTINUED OVERLEAF

cooking further. Once cool, transfer them to a tray and lightly oil each sheet to stop them sticking to one another.

Turn your oven up to 220°C fan while you assemble the lasagne. Start with a layer of béchamel, followed by a layer of lasagne sheets, a scattering of pumpkin, some roughly torn mozzarella and a touch of grated parmesan. Repeat these layers, pressing down the lasagne sheets with each layer. Finish with a final lid of lasagne sheets and a very generous layer of béchamel.

Place in the oven and bake for 20–30 minutes, until golden brown on top, being careful it doesn't burn. Let the lasagne cool for 15 minutes before tucking in. This one's a winner – enjoy!

EGG CURRY
with coconut sambal & flatbreads

IF YOU'VE NEVER HAD AN EGG CURRY BEFORE, LET ME INTRODUCE YOU. This is an ideal start to a winter's day, comforting and warming, with enough zing and spice to put a lasting pep in your step. This dish is inspired by the egg curries of Sri Lanka and southern India, and is coconut based, which adds a sweet richness, with a little tomato for acidity and lots of ginger and green chillies for their warming heat. Coconut sambal is a grated coconut side that you get all over Sri Lanka, made with shredded coconut, herbs, lime and chillies, providing a wonderful freshness against the richer flavours of a curry. Traditionally it's made with freshly grated coconut, but I find desiccated coconut works well enough when freshened up with a splash of water. I like this curry pretty spicy, so I use green bird's-eye chillies, seeds and all, but if you want to tone it down a bit, remove the seeds. With the sambal, go big on the lime – it wants to be explosively fresh and zingy. Serve with warm flatbreads or roti.

SERVES 4

for the curry paste

3 cloves of garlic

2 thumbs of fresh ginger

1 tbsp coconut oil

5 green cardamom pods

½ stick of cinnamon

2 tsp coriander seeds

1 tsp cumin seeds

1 tsp ground turmeric

½ tsp mustard seeds

for the curry base

1 large brown onion

2 green chillies

1 tbsp coconut oil

CONT. OVERLEAF

For the curry paste, smash and peel the garlic, then peel and roughly chop the ginger. Heat the coconut oil in a small pan. Once warm, add the spices, garlic and ginger and fry on a medium heat for a minute or two until fragrant, being incredibly careful they don't burn. Transfer to a Nutribullet/food processor with a splash of water and blitz to a fine paste. Season with a pinch of salt and set aside.

For the curry base, finely slice the onion and cut the chillies into thirds on the diagonal. Heat the coconut oil in a heavy-based pan and, once warm, add the curry leaves and chillies. Fry briefly until they sizzle and release their fragrance, then add the onion with a decent pinch of salt. Cook for 8–10 minutes, until the onion begins to caramelise at the edges. Lift 4 tomatoes from the tin and crush them into the pan – I know it seems weird not to just use the whole tin, but the flavour would take over. Add the curry paste and cook for 5 minutes, stirring regularly. Now add the coconut milk and cook for 15 minutes, until the flavours have melded and the sauce has thickened. Have a taste and adjust the seasoning as necessary.

CONTINUED OVERLEAF

10 fresh curry leaves

*1 x 400g tin of plum
tomatoes*

*1 x 400ml tin of coconut
milk*

8 eggs

for the coconut sambal

*100g desiccated coconut (or
even better, freshly grated
coconut)*

1 small brown onion

30g fresh coriander

1 green chilli (optional)

juice of 1 lime

salt and a sprinkle of sugar

for serving

warm flatbreads

While the curry is coming together, get a large pan of water on to a rolling boil and add the eggs. We're aiming for medium soft-boiled here with lovely jammy yolks. So set a timer for 7 minutes, and when they're ready, remove and plunge into cold water. Peel off the shells and add the eggs to the curry sauce.

To make the sambal, pour the coconut into a bowl and grate in the onion. Pour a few splashes of water over the coconut and stir together, adding more until it loses its dryness. Finely chop the coriander and chilli, if using, and stir through the coconut, being careful with the chilli at first. At this point have a taste, and season generously with lime, sugar and salt until you're happy. Add more green chilli bit by bit to find the right level of spice for you.

Serve the curry in bowls, with warm flatbreads and a generous amount of the coconut sambal. Delicious at all times of the day, particularly as a late breakfast – add rice if you want to bulk it out for lunch.

FISH PIE

FIND ME A DISH MORE SOOTHING THAN A STEAMING BOWL OF FISH PIE. A timeless classic for a reason, it takes me straight back to my childhood. But like so many of these old favourites, it's worth taking time over to really make it sing. My advice is to keep the fish in quite large pieces that go into the pie raw, so that when cooked they flake into succulent chunks. The sauce is the key that holds it all together, infused with a smoky richness from the haddock and a light touch of lemon zest. I like huge handfuls of parsley and tons of tarragon, and you won't find any boiled eggs or rubbery prawns here. To finish, pillows of buttery mash that barely hold together and melt into the sauce below. When done right it really is a masterful thing. This is a large pie, great for feeding a crowd, or whack half in the freezer for a rainy day.

SERVES 8–10

550ml whole milk

250ml double cream

2 bay leaves

a few sprigs of fresh thyme

1 brown onion

400g undyed smoked
  haddock

3 large leeks

1kg fish (I like to use 600g
  pollack and 400g trout)

20g fresh parsley

20g fresh tarragon leaves

80g butter

300g spinach

40g plain flour

150ml white wine or
  vermouth

1 unwaxed lemon

CONT. OVERLEAF

First, pour the milk and cream into a wide pan. Add the bay leaves, thyme and quartered onion with a few generous turns of black pepper and bring this up to a gentle simmer to infuse. After 5 minutes, turn the heat right down and place in the haddock. Let the fish cook gently for 5 minutes, then remove and while it's still warm, peel off the skin and flake the fish into large pieces, watching out for any bones. Leave to cool on a plate and strain the smoky milk mixture through a sieve into a bowl. Chop the leeks into chunky 2cm rounds. Skin and bone the rest of the fish, then chop into large chunks (you can ask your fishmonger to do this for you). Finely chop the parsley and tarragon.

Add 40g of butter to the pan you cooked the haddock in and melt gently, then add the leeks with a little splash of water and season well with salt. Put the lid on the pan and cook the leeks slowly and carefully, until they're sweet and tender without taking on any colour. Wash the spinach and add to the leeks, season again and cook until the spinach has barely wilted, then pour into a sieve and leave to drain. Now, over a medium heat, add the remaining 40g of butter to the same pan, and once melted add the flour and whisk together.

CONTINUED OVERLEAF

for the mash

1.3kg Maris Piper potatoes

250ml whole milk

250g butter

1 tbsp Dijon mustard

some grated Gruyère
  (optional)

Cook for a few minutes, until the flour is thick and smells a little biscuity, then pour in the wine and whisk to combine. Add the smoky milk and cream mixture a ladleful at a time, thoroughly whisking in each ladleful before adding the next. When the sauce has come together, turn the heat off and have a taste. Season well with salt and pepper, squeeze in a touch of lemon and grate in some zest. It should be delicious, so take the time to make it so. Add the spinach, leeks, parsley and tarragon and mix to combine.

To make the mash, peel the potatoes and cut into large even chunks. Place in a pan, cover with cold water and season well. Bring up to a simmer and cook until the potatoes are soft and can be easily skewered with a knife. Strain and leave in a colander to steam for 5 minutes. In the meantime, put the milk into a small pan with 200g of butter and place on a medium heat to melt. Mash the potatoes or pass through a ricer, then add the milk and butter and mix to combine. To season, add the mustard and lots of pepper, then taste and adjust as necessary. This is the stage where you can add an optional grating of Gruyère.

Preheat your oven to 200°C fan.

Now to assemble! Arrange the pieces of pollack, trout and haddock on the bottom of your chosen dish and season with salt. Pour over the sauce and shake the dish so it spreads evenly through the fish. Now cover carefully with the mash, placing it at the sides first rather than pushing it into the sauce, then fill in the middle. Rough the top with a fork and dot with the remaining 50g of butter. Place in the oven for about 20–30 minutes, until the sauce is bubbling and the potato has taken on a touch of gold. Serve immediately, piping hot and steaming. It shouldn't need anything other than a crack of pepper over the top.

CHICKEN, LEEK & TARRAGON PIE

ONE OF LIFE'S GREAT PLEASURES IS A WELL-MADE CHICKEN PIE. Rich and comforting, if I ever need help on the farm, this is the dish I make in order to persuade my brothers, who will do almost anything in return. Buttery, flaky, fennel-spiked pastry with a mustard-heavy leek and tarragon filling . . . it's utter heaven. I like to use a whole quality chicken, which makes enough for two pies so you have a spare for the freezer – such a treat to pull out on a rainy day. But if you would like to make a smaller amount, use 6–8 chicken thighs and halve the recipe. It's quite a process, but a peaceful and methodical one, so settle in and enjoy – the end result is more than worth it. (*Pictured overleaf.*)

MAKES 2 MEDIUM PIES,
EACH ONE SERVING 4

to poach the chicken

1 quality chicken (better the
  chicken, better the pie)

olive oil, for frying

1 brown onion

2 celery sticks

1 carrot

3 bay leaves

for the pie

3 celery sticks

3 large leeks

6 rashers of the best smoked
  streaky bacon you can find

30g butter

600ml poaching broth from
  the chicken

50g plain flour

a generous glass of white
  wine (150ml)

200ml double cream

CONT. OVERLEAF

Start by cutting the chicken in two lengthways; you can ask your butcher to do this for you, but it's very easy to do yourself. Take a pair of kitchen scissors or shears and cut along one side of the spine as if you were spatchcocking the chicken. Then do the same down the breast. Season generously all over and leave for about an hour for the salt to penetrate. After the hour, get a large heavy-based pot that ideally fits both halves of the chicken, drizzle in a splash of oil and crank up the heat. When the oil is shimmering, fry the two pieces of chicken on both sides until golden brown all over – the more caramelisation the better. You can do this in two batches if your pot isn't quite big enough to take both pieces of chicken in a single layer. When the chicken is browned, roughly chop the veg and chuck in with the bay leaves. Top up with water so that the chicken is just covered. Season generously with salt and bring up to the gentlest of simmers with the lid on for 30 minutes, until the chicken is just cooked through.

When ready, remove the chicken from the pot and leave to cool. When cool enough to handle (I whack on a pair of Marigolds), strip the chicken meat from the carcass and place it in a bowl, making sure to get the meat from every nook and cranny. I like the skin in my pie, but if you don't, put it back into the stock pot along with all the bones and gristle. Put this pan back on the heat and simmer to

CONTINUED OVERLEAF

1 heaped tbsp Dijon mustard

20g fresh tarragon

1 egg

*2 sheets of all-butter puff
  pastry, or homemade rough
  puff pastry (see page 310)*

fennel seeds

extract all the goodness from the bones while you get on
with the rest of the cooking. This stock is what forms the
sauce, so you want it to be good.

Halve the sticks of celery lengthways and slice, then
chop the leeks into 2cm rounds. Remove any rind from the
bacon before cutting into chunks, then place in a large pan
with the butter and fry to render out the fat. Add the celery
and leeks along with a ladle of the chicken stock, then put
the lid on and slowly cook until completely tender. Take care
not to break up the leeks too much – you want to retain their
shape as much as possible.

At this point, strain the chicken stock and measure out
600ml. Taste the stock and season with salt as necessary.
Add the flour to the leeks and mix well, cooking for a few
minutes, until the flour smells a little biscuity, then pour in
the wine and mix again to create a claggy mess. Now add the
chicken stock a ladle at a time, stirring until it is completely
mixed in before adding the next ladle; this ensures there are
no lumps. When all the chicken stock has been added, turn
off the heat and pour in the cream. Add the chicken meat,
mustard and finely chopped tarragon. Mix thoroughly and
taste – adjust the seasoning until it's perfect. You may want a
bit more mustard, but be careful, as it can quickly take over.

This mix makes enough for two medium-sized pies. I
get my pie dish and fill it for 4 people, then I freeze the rest
in another dish as a ready-to-go pastry-topped pie, which
is such a treat to have in the freezer. Preheat your oven to
200°C fan. Whisk an egg and brush the rim of your dish.
Place the rolled-out pastry on top and crimp the edges. I like
to leave a generous overhang, but if there's any excess, use
this to make some decorations for the top of the pie. Brush
the top with more egg wash, then sprinkle with fennel seeds
and season with salt and pepper. Pierce a hole in the middle
for the steam to escape, then place in the oven for about
30 minutes, until the top is golden brown and puffed.

HEARTY SAUSAGE STEW
with beans, Swiss chard & cinnamon

THIS IS A DISH I OFTEN FIND MYSELF YEARNING FOR on a long, dark evening. It sits somewhere between a soup and a stew. As the beans cook they relax into the unctuous broth, studded with rosemary, chilli and cinnamon for a soothing warmth. If you can find Italian sausages, they have a coarser texture and pleasing richness, but a quality British banger will do the trick too. We eat this on our knees by the fire with rain lashing against the windows. All it needs is a hunk of bread with butter thick enough to leave teeth marks.

SERVES 4–5

500g Italian sausages

3 cloves of garlic

2 celery sticks

2 brown onions

3 tbsp olive oil

a generous pinch of chilli
flakes, for warmth, not
prickly heat

a few sprigs of rosemary
(sage or thyme also work)

2 bay leaves

1 stick of cinnamon

a small glass of Madeira,
sweetish sherry, beer or
white wine

2 plum tomatoes from a tin

1 x 700g jar of white beans
(or 2 x 400g tins – I like
to use 1 cannellini and
1 butter bean)

750ml chicken stock
(see page 306)

250g Swiss chard or
cavolo nero

Start by slicing the skin of the sausages so you can remove the meat. Then roughly break into small meatball-size pieces. Finely slice the garlic, celery and onions. Get a large heavy-based pan hot, drizzle in the olive oil and, once warm, add the sausage. Fry for a few minutes to release the fat and get some colour on the meat. Then turn the heat right down and add the garlic, chilli flakes, rosemary, bay leaves and cinnamon. Don't let the garlic take on any colour – this stage is about slowly infusing flavour into the oil, so you want a low heat and a gentle sizzle.

When ready, pour in the Madeira to deglaze the pan – you can do this early, to cool down the pan if your garlic is beginning to colour. With a wooden spoon, scrape up all the goodness from the bottom of the pan, then add the onions and celery, and crush in the tomatoes. Season generously, mix well and cook on a gentle heat for 10–12 minutes, until the onions are sweet and wonderfully softened.

Add the beans and pour in the stock. Bring to a gentle simmer, then cook for about 20–30 minutes, until the broth thickens and the flavours come together.

Strip the stalks from the Swiss chard and chop into 2cm pieces. Add them to the broth and simmer for a few minutes, then add the leaves and stir through. Put the lid on, turn off the heat and leave for 5 minutes. When ready, remove the lid and have a taste. You might want to add a touch more chilli flakes if the warmth isn't quite there, and more salt if the broth isn't rich enough. Pour generously into bowls and serve with thick slices of lavishly buttered bread for dunking.

LAMB WITH ANCHOVY & ROSEMARY
on a bed of beans braised with Swiss chard

THIS ANCHOVY AND ROSEMARY SAUCE BECAME A BIT OF AN OBSESSION of mine this year. It's incredibly simple to make, rich with anchovy and lifted by the zing from the rosemary and lemon. Great on grilled chicken thighs or roasted radicchio (or any veg for that matter), but utter heaven against the fattiness of lamb.

Swiss chard is one of the easiest things to grow, and though I plant it every year, I never quite knew what to do with it. This autumn, I went to a neighbour's for lunch and one of the things he served was boiled Swiss chard with nothing but salt and a drizzle of olive oil. I understood it then, finally awaking to the simple joy in the pleasing crunch of the stalks and mineral-rich leaves dressed in peppery olive oil. And ever since, the chard in my garden has been picked bare. I'll be planting double the amount next year and, if you have a veg patch, I encourage you to do the same. If you can't find it, cavolo nero, kale and spinach are great replacements for this recipe.

SERVES 4

1 rack of lamb

450g Swiss chard

3 cloves of garlic

3 tbsp olive oil

*1 x 700g jar of white beans
(or 2 x 400g tins – I like
to use 1 cannellini and
1 butter bean)*

1 unwaxed lemon

for the rosemary and
anchovy sauce

3 sprigs of rosemary

*12 salted anchovies
(about 1 tin)*

60ml olive oil

juice of ½ lemon

Sprinkle the lamb generously with salt and leave on a plate to come to room temperature. To make the rosemary and anchovy sauce, put the rosemary leaves, anchovies and olive oil into a high-speed blender and blitz until smooth. Taste, then add a squeeze of lemon, blitz again and have another taste – keep adjusting until you get the balance right. I usually find it wants about half a lemon, but once I did just that and it turned out to be a really strong lemon and ruined the sauce. A great lesson, I had to double the batch just to mellow out the acidity. So add slowly, tasting as you go.

When the salt has penetrated the lamb, preheat your oven to 180°C fan. Get a large frying pan hot and place the lamb skin side down. Fry slowly until the fat renders and becomes crisp and caramelised – you want a deep brown colour. Turn over and briefly brown the other side, then place on a tray in the oven. For lamb that's pink in the middle, cook for 10–20 minutes or until the centre of the meat is 50°C, then remove and leave to rest for 10 minutes with a bit of foil on top. By the time the lamb has rested, the internal temperature will have increased to 55°C, which is perfect.

CONTINUED OVERLEAF

If you don't have a temperature probe, prod the middle of the meat – if it's still squishy it's not quite ready. You're looking for medium-firm but with some give, much like a steak. If it's completely firm, I'm afraid you've gone too far. Keep in mind that all pieces of lamb are different, as well as the heat of your oven and the thickness of your pan, so use these timings as a rough guide.

While the lamb is cooking, separate the chard leaves from the stalks. Roughly cut the stalks and tear the leaves into smaller pieces. Finely slice the garlic. Put a heavy-based pan on a medium heat, drizzle in the olive oil and, once warm, add the garlic. Gently sizzle to infuse the oil, then pour in the beans (with their liquid if using jarred – drain and rinse if using tinned), season and bring up to a simmer. If using jarred beans (my preference here), all that's needed is to bring them up to a simmer, as they are already soft and ready to go. You may need to add a splash or two of water if there isn't enough liquid. I find tins need about 30 minutes of extra cooking to make them tender, so if using tins, add a tin's worth of water and gently simmer with the lid on until the beans are soft. I sometimes squish a few of them with a potato masher just to thicken the sauce if it needs it.

Grate in the lemon zest, then stir through the chard stalks and make sure there is enough liquid to cover them. Gently simmer until the stalks are tender, about 3–5 minutes, then add the leaves and mix them through – they will take no time at all to cook. Turn the heat off and squeeze in a splash of lemon juice, then grind in some pepper and mix well. Have a taste and adjust the seasoning as necessary. Carve up the lamb – hopefully it should be beautifully pink – add a generous scoop of beans to each plate, then top with the lamb and finish with the rosemary and anchovy sauce.

BRAISED SHORT RIBS

SHORT RIBS ARE ONE OF THE GREAT CUTS FOR SLOW COOKING, as they're generously marbled with fat, which melts as they cook, yielding ludicrously tender meat. Spooned over a bed of parmesan-enriched polenta and finished with a handful of parsley, this is lip-smackingly good, deeply comforting and easy to execute. This recipe makes quite a large quantity and I'd keep it that way, as it's great freezer fodder; knowing there's a batch of this ready provides solace in biting weather. It also makes a fantastic ragu if you shred the meat off the bones. Just cook the pasta until it's a few minutes off being ready. Then strain and chuck into a warm pan of the sauce, adding a generous splash of starchy pasta water and lashings of parmesan. Mix vigorously to bind the richly flavoured sauce and finish with a generous handful of finely chopped parsley. (*Pictured overleaf.*)

SERVES 8–10

about 1.5kg beef short ribs

8 brown onions

4 carrots

4 celery sticks

olive oil

1 tbsp tomato purée

5 anchovies (optional – you won't taste them, but they add so much depth)

150ml red wine

1 x 400g tin of plum tomatoes

300ml whole milk

3 bay leaves, a small bunch of fresh thyme and a sprig of fresh sage, tied in a bundle

½ nutmeg

a bunch of fresh parsley

wet polenta, for serving (double the recipe on page 144)

Season the ribs generously with salt and set aside for half an hour to come to room temperature. Meanwhile, very thinly slice the onions. Peel, quarter and slice the carrots, and dice the celery. Once the meat has lost the chill of the fridge, heat a large heavy-based ovenproof pan with a splash of oil and fry in batches, until deeply caramelised all over. Remove from the pan and set aside.

Return the pan to a medium heat, then fry the onions with a generous pinch of salt in the fat rendered from the beef. The onions should release some liquid as they fry; use this to scrape any beef caramelisation from the bottom of the pan. When the onions have softened, add the carrots and celery, fry for a further 10 minutes, then make a well in the middle and add the tomato purée and anchovies, if using, to the bottom of the pan. Mix and crush so they melt, then stir among the veg. At this stage, preheat your oven to 140°C fan.

CONTINUED OVERLEAF

Keep cooking the veg for another 5 minutes, until they're beginning to stick but not brown – this is a sign that you've cooked off enough of the water and that they're beginning to caramelise. Add the wine and cook off the alcohol. Add the tinned tomatoes, smushing each tomato in your hand on its way into the pan, then add the milk and the bundle of herbs and grate in the nutmeg. Season generously with salt and pepper, then add the meat to the pan and nestle it into the liquid. Bring back to a gentle simmer. Cut a circle of baking parchment to the size of the pan and press this into the meat so it sticks to the top and forms a seal. Then put the lid on and place in the oven for 3 hours, until the meat is completely tender.

When ready, remove from the oven. A lot of fat will have rendered from the beef, which is what keeps it so tender. But now it's done its job, you can remove it. If eating straight away, use a ladle or large spoon to skim it off, being careful not to remove too much of the sauce. A little bit of fat is great, but too much is excessive. If you're not eating straight away, allow the dish to cool and place in the fridge. The fat will solidify and becomes easy to remove. Often slow-cooked dishes are better the next day anyway.

To serve, make sure to have a final taste and carefully adjust the seasoning as necessary. Serve on the bone over a puddle of creamy polenta with lots of the sauce and a smattering of parsley.

PORK BELLY BRAISED IN CIDER
with onions & prunes

ONE OF MY FAVOURITE RESTAURANTS IN LONDON, Koya, has the most divine dish of cider-braised pork belly on their menu, which I've been obsessed with for years. The pork is slow-cooked in cider with soy, mirin and sugar until it thickens into a sticky glaze that coats the almost jellified pork. Sadly, being rather tied to the farm, it's a dish I don't get to eat as often as I'd like, so with inspiration from Fergus and Margot Henderson and their love of pork and prunes, I started to have a play, trying to find a wintry version that I could cook at home with local ingredients. This is the result – slow-cooked pork belly from just down the road with homemade cider and milk from my neighbour, tons of onions and prunes with a bundle of sage. The result is a heavenly sauce with impossibly tender pork that bursts with flavour. Finished with a balancing splash of soy as a nod to Koya and served on a bed of buttery mash, this has become a dish I often yearn for.

SERVES 6–8

1kg piece of pork belly, bones removed

4 large brown onions

5 cloves of garlic

2 tbsp sunflower oil

500ml medium dry cider

250ml whole milk or chicken stock (see page 306)

200g pitted prunes

5 sprigs of fresh sage

a generous pinch of ground mace or ½ nutmeg

a splash of soy, to taste

Season the pork belly generously all over and leave for at least half an hour for the salt to penetrate. Finely slice the onions and garlic. When the pork belly is ready, put a large heavy-based pan that's wide enough to fit the meat on to a medium-high heat. If you don't have a pan big enough, cut the pork in half and cook in two batches. Drizzle in a splash of sunflower oil, pat the skin dry, then place the pork skin side down and fry until golden brown, being careful it doesn't burn. When the skin is golden, flip and fry the other side until caramelised. When it's golden all over, remove from the pan and transfer to a chopping board. Turn the heat down and add the onions and garlic with a generous pinch of salt and a splash of water. Cook slowly for about 15 minutes, until really sweet and beginning to caramelise, being careful the onions don't burn – add a splash more water if they're beginning to catch.

While the onions are cooking, cut the pork into strips about the thickness of your thumb. When the onions are ready, pour in the cider and deglaze the pan. Then add the milk, prunes, sage and mace. Nestle the pork in and among the onions and prunes, making sure it's submerged, adding more milk if needed. Season again with lots of pepper

CONTINUED OVERLEAF

and a generous pinch of salt. Then cut a piece of baking parchment to the size of the pan and press it on to the pork so it sticks to the liquid and creates a seal. Bring the pan up to the gentlest of simmers so that it's barely bubbling, then put the lid on and leave to cook for 2 hours.

When the 2 hours are up, remove the baking parchment and see if you can push the side of a fork or butter knife through the pork – it should be incredibly tender. Get a spoon and have a taste of the broth; it should be fantastic, but I find a tiny touch of soy brings it home and darkens the colour a little. When you have the seasoning perfect – remembering that soy is salty, so be careful with any salt additions, and adding a touch more spice if you think it needs it – place the baking parchment back on the pork and leave to rest. You could make this the day before if you like, it will only improve overnight. Serve the pork piping hot, with plenty of the prunes and sauce. All it needs is some buttery mash and winter greens on the side.

APPLE TURNOVERS

FROM LATE AUGUST THROUGH TO JANUARY WE ARE BOMBARDED by an endless supply of apples. The farm is surrounded by twisted lichen-covered trees that stand like old men leaning on their canes in every nook and cranny. We have cookers and eaters of many flavours and colours, and from October each gust of wind sends a carpet to the ground in a riot of colour. We fill endless wheelbarrows for the goats and sheep, collect them by the bucket for juicing, make barrels of cider and munch on them for breakfast, lunch and dinner, yet still we hardly make a dent. They find their way into stews, meatballs, crumbles and pies. But of the many dishes they are used in, this is an old favourite. Play around with the spices, add a splash of brandy or ginger, orange zest, raisins and almonds . . . just remember to give them a minute to cool before you tuck in, or the lava within will incinerate your tongue.

This makes extra filling that can be used on porridge, yoghurt or even atop some ice cream as a quick pudding. Even better, what I do is make twelve turnovers with two sheets of puff pastry. You can freeze six for a rainy day, then egg wash and bake from frozen, adding an extra 10 minutes or so to the cooking time. (*Pictured overleaf.*)

MAKES 6 TURNOVERS

4 medium cooking apples

30g butter

1 tsp ground cinnamon

½ nutmeg, grated

a pinch of ground cloves

100g soft brown sugar

2 tsp cornflour

1 eating apple

1 unwaxed lemon

1 sheet of puff pastry, or homemade rough puff pastry (see page 310)

1 egg

demerara sugar, for sprinkling

double cream, ice cream or crème fraîche, for serving

Peel the cooking apples and cut them into quarters, then remove the cores and halve each quarter. Place a pan on a medium heat and add the cooking apples along with the butter, spices and brown sugar. Cook gently until the apples are tender and enveloped in a sticky sauce, but don't let them turn to mush, texture is important. If you find they're sticking to the bottom of the pan, add a little splash of water, but go carefully as you don't want the mixture to become too runny. After 10–15 minutes, mix the cornflour with 2 teaspoons of water and add to the apple, cook for a few minutes until the sauce thickens, then turn off the heat. At this point, peel and cube the eating apple and stir it through the cooked apple – this provides a lovely change of texture later on. Grate in the zest of the lemon and squeeze in the juice of half, then taste and adjust with the rest of the lemon juice as needed. Leave to cool.

Roll out a sheet of puff pastry on a piece of baking parchment and cut into six squares. Place a generous dollop of the cooled apple mixture on one half of each square, leaving a 1.5cm edge to seal the pastry later on. I find this is a constant battle between wanting as much apple as possible and not overfilling, so they can still be sealed. Don't worry if they're not immaculate, mine never are.

Whisk the egg, brush the edges of the pastry and fold over the other half to form a triangle. Pinch together or press with a fork to seal, then poke a few holes in the top to let out the steam. Transfer to a baking tray and place in the fridge while you preheat your oven to 200°C fan.

Remove from the fridge and brush the tops with egg wash, then place in the oven and cook for 20–30 minutes, until the pastry is a deep golden brown. When ready, remove from the oven and sprinkle with demerara sugar. Leave to cool for 10 minutes, and serve with your favourite form of cream.

GINGER CAKE, POACHED QUINCE
& CRÈME FRAÎCHE

THANKS TO A LATE FROST, OUR QUINCE TREE DIDN'T FRUIT LAST YEAR. But this autumn, it more than made up for it and hung heavy with the luminous and richly perfumed fruit. As objects, quince are a work of art, making wonderful decorations on the windowsills of the house, where they glow in the light and fill the room with their dizzying, floral scent. While you can eat quinces raw, they're at their best when cooked or preserved. They make the original 'marmalade', a great jelly to go with cheese, and are unbelievable infused into vodka – I have 8 litres steeping as I write and the aroma is astonishing. But perhaps best of all, quince can be gently poached so they take on a rose colour and a sweet but sharp flavour that is just sheer joy. A recent trip to our great local restaurant Brassica reminded me of an old recipe in my granny's notebook for a sticky spiced ginger cake. Here, served as they do, with crème fraîche, the poached quince and lots of their cooking liquor, making quite the winter pudding.

SERVES 8–10

for the ginger cake

150g dark muscovado sugar
250g black treacle
150g unsalted butter
2 tsp ground ginger
1 tsp ground cinnamon
½ tsp ground cloves
¼ tsp ground black pepper
50g grated fresh ginger
280ml whole milk
2 eggs
300g plain flour
1½ tsp baking powder
1 tsp bicarbonate of soda

to poach the quince

2 litres water
300g caster sugar
8 ripe quinces
1 lemon
crème fraîche, for serving

Preheat your oven to 130°C fan.

Start with the quinces. Bring the water to the boil, add the caster sugar and stir to dissolve, then keep warm. Peel and either halve or quarter the quinces, then remove the cores with a sharp teaspoon or paring knife (I find an oyster knife particularly good for this). Keep all the peelings and offcuts, as these help bring out the best colour from the quince. Place the quince quarters at the bottom of an ovenproof pan, then cover with all the peelings. Squeeze in the lemon juice and pour over the hot sugar syrup. Place a piece of baking parchment on top, then cover with a plate to submerge the quinces and place a lid on the pan. Put in the oven for 3–4 hours, until the quinces are rose-coloured and tender but not falling apart.

Remove the quinces from the oven and leave to cool, submerged in the syrup. When cold, remove all the peelings but keep the quinces submerged in syrup and place in the fridge, where they will keep happily for quite a while. Poached quince are sublime in a crumble, in frangipane tarts (page 289), with yoghurt, as in my plum recipe (page 284), all sorts of things. Serve them with lots of the syrup, but if you have any leftover liquid, it makes a fantastic cordial, cocktail or even sorbet.

CONTINUED OVERLEAF

Preheat your oven to 170°C fan.

To make the ginger cake, start by lining a baking tin 28cm x 20cm and 5cm deep with baking parchment. (You can use a slightly smaller tin than this, but anything larger will result in a thinner cake.) Put the muscovado sugar, treacle, butter, spices and fresh ginger into a pan and place on a medium heat to dissolve. When molten, mix together and leave to cool for 15 minutes. Then add the milk, followed by the eggs, and mix again. Stir the flour with the baking powder and bicarbonate of soda to make sure they're evenly dispersed, then sift the flour into the treacle mix and bring together, mixing thoroughly to ensure there are no lumps. Pour the runny batter into your prepared baking tin, then place in the oven and bake for 45 minutes–1 hour, until risen and cooked through. To test, insert a skewer into the middle of the cake – if it comes out clean, you're good to go. Leave to cool for 15 minutes before slicing, then serve warm with crème fraîche, poached quince and lots of the syrup.

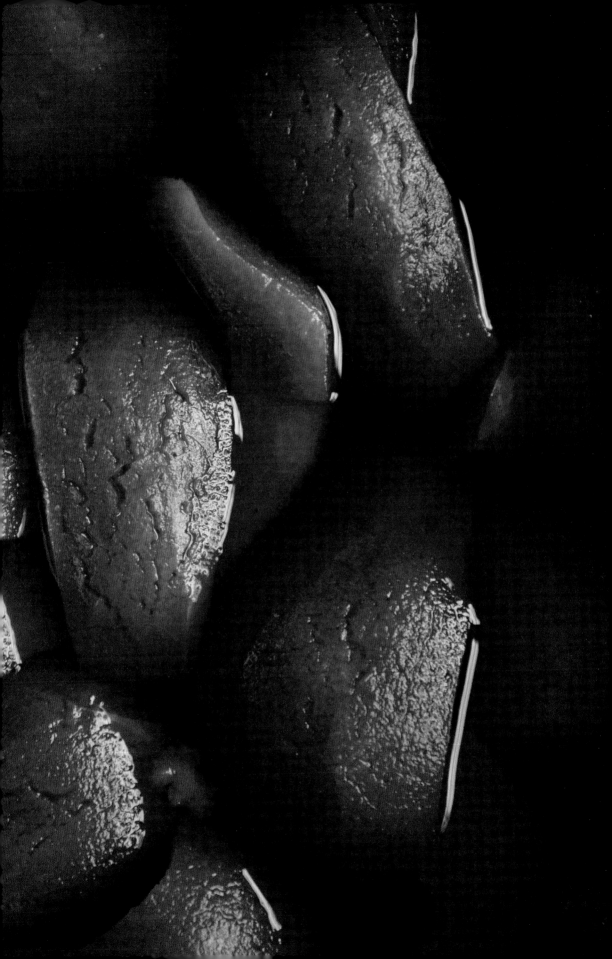

PEAR & WALNUT UPSIDE-DOWN CAKE

I LOVE A GOOD CAKE AND THIS IS JUST THAT. Juicy, moist and wonderfully light, but most importantly, not too sweet. It sings with warm flavours from the spices, while the walnuts provide an earthy and satisfying crunch. The pears are first cooked in a caramel until sweet and tender, and you then pour the batter over and bake the cake upside down. Once cooked, you turn out the cake and let the caramel trickle into the sponge below. All it needs is a spoon of crème fraîche and you will be happy as can be. I find this cake lasts a good few days, especially if you keep it covered. Just gently warm any leftover slices in a low 140°C fan oven before you tuck in, which brings it back to life.

MAKES 8 SLICES

for the caramelised pear topping
6 ripe pears
50g butter
80g soft brown sugar
juice of 1½ lemons

for the cake
200g butter, softened
200g caster sugar
4 eggs
seeds from 5 cardamom pods
3 cloves
100g walnuts
200g self-raising flour
4 tsp baking powder
5g sea salt
1 tsp ground cinnamon
100g sour cream

for serving
crème fraîche or double cream

Start by peeling the pears, then cut into quarters lengthways and remove the cores with a sharp knife. Place a wide frying pan on a medium heat and add the butter. When it begins to melt, add the pears, cut side down, then sprinkle the soft brown sugar over the top and shimmy the pan, using the weight of the pears to mix the sugar into the butter. Squeeze in the lemon juice and cook down for 8–10 minutes, until the pears have softened and the butter and sugar have become an amber-coloured caramel. Remove the pears and arrange cut side up, fat side out in a 9-inch cake tin (you may not need all of them). Ideally don't use a springform tin, as the small gap allows the caramel to trickle out. But if you have to, use some baking parchment to create a seal (if possible, you want the cake touching the metal sides as this creates a lovely crust). Leave the caramel bubbling on a low heat to reduce further until it is properly thick, then pour over the pears.

Preheat your oven to 180°C fan.

For the cake, you can either mix with an electric whisk or use a stand mixer. Place the softened butter in a large bowl and add the sugar. Whisk until the butter is pale and fluffy, scraping down the sides a few times to make sure it is evenly incorporated. With the mixer running, add the eggs one at a time, making sure each one is thoroughly mixed before adding the next, or the butter may split.

CONTINUED OVERLEAF

Grind the cardamom seeds and cloves in a pestle and mortar, then pour into a bowl. Bash the walnuts in the pestle and mortar or crush them in a folded tea towel, using a rolling pin. You want to keep a chunky texture. Mix the flour with the baking powder to ensure it's evenly distributed. Sift, then add to the butter with the salt, cinnamon, ground spices and walnuts. Mix these dry ingredients into the batter, then stir through the sour cream. Pour the cake batter over the pears and lightly even out the top.

Now, remembering that all ovens are different, place in the middle of your oven for up to an hour, until the cake is set. After around 30 minutes, I turn the heat down to 160°C fan to make sure the top doesn't get too dark. Keep an eye, but don't open the door or you risk the cake deflating. After about 50 minutes, give the cake a jiggle – if the middle is at all wobbly it's not cooked yet. To test, insert a skewer into the middle and when it comes out clean it's ready.

At this point, remove from the oven and leave to sit for 15 minutes, then place a chopping board gently on top of the cake. Flip the cake and board, then remove the tin and you should have a beautifully risen cake with juicy caramelised pears on top. I like to serve it warm, with crème fraîche or double cream and a coffee. It stays juicy for a good few days – just warm up a slice in the oven at 140°C fan.

CHOCOLATE MOUSSE
with spiced Armagnac prunes

THIS MOUSSE IS AN OLD ELIZABETH DAVID RECIPE, an exercise in purist perfection that I couldn't live without, just 30g of chocolate and 1 egg per person. It goes beautifully with these Armagnac prunes, which I make every Christmas. If you can start them a week in advance that's good going, but the flavour after they've infused for a month is just incredible, great to have in the cupboard as a ready-to-go pudding when needed. I've made the recipe for four, but the prunes make a pretty hefty jar that will last you a while. Try them with crème fraîche, walnuts and a generous ladle of the liquor, but also chopped up over ice cream, or even better *in* homemade ice cream. (*Pictured overleaf.*)

SERVES 4

for the chocolate mousse

120g dark chocolate, 70%

4 eggs

for the Armagnac prunes

3 Earl Grey teabags

800g–1kg pitted prunes

zest of 1 large orange

1 stick of cinnamon

5 star anise

10 cloves

700ml Armagnac, or any good brandy

200g caster sugar

for serving

crème fraîche and flaky sea salt

Start with the prunes. Boil a kettle and pour 1 litre of water into a pan or bowl, then chuck in the teabags and leave to infuse for 5 minutes. Remove the bags, giving them a squeeze, then add the prunes. Leave to steep until the water is completely cold, or even better overnight. Strain the prunes and place in a large Kilner jar. Peel in the orange zest and add the spices, then cover with the brandy and add the sugar. Close the lid, hold it tight and shake to mix through the sugar and spices. These will now keep for a very long time as long as they're submerged in the brandy, and the longer you leave them, the better they get.

To make the mousse, break the chocolate and place in a heatproof bowl with 4 tablespoons of water. Suspend this bowl over a bain-marie (a pan of gently simmering water) and slowly warm the chocolate until it melts. Don't stir, just let it do its thing. When molten, stir to combine the chocolate with the water until it forms a smooth ganache – you can add another tablespoon of water if it's not silky enough. Separate the egg yolks from the whites, putting the whites into a large mixing bowl. When the chocolate has cooled down a little, add the yolks and mix together until well combined. If it splits rather than staying smooth, add a tablespoon of water at a time, stirring vigorously until smooth and silky.

CONTINUED OVERLEAF

Now whisk the whites by hand until they form stiff peaks. I used to always use a machine, but . . . only realised recently that you can actually overwhisk an egg white, resulting in a kind of grainy, clumpy foam that is hard to mix into whatever you're making, compared to a smooth and silky foam that mixes through wonderfully. Personally, I find you have much more control whisking by hand, but you can use a machine if you like, just keep a close eye and turn it off to test the consistency until you think it's right. What you're looking for is, when you lift your whisk out of the egg whites, they leave behind a thin meringue-like spike that stands with a gentle curve. Take a third of the whipped egg whites and fold them into the chocolate in a gentle figure-of-eight, making sure there are no flecks. Then gently add the rest, this time being particularly careful not to knock any air out of the whites as you fold them into the chocolate. The first third loosens the chocolate enough so that with the remaining two-thirds you can be especially diligent and maximise the air. Spoon the mousse either into one bowl, or individual ramekins/glasses, then cover and leave in the fridge for at least a few hours, until set.

Serve a spoon of the chocolate mousse per person, add 3 prunes and a generous pool of the flavoured brandy. Finish with a spoon of crème fraîche and scatter a pinch of flaky salt over the chocolate.

ORANGE VODKA

ONE YEAR I BOUGHT AN AMBITIOUS AMOUNT OF ORANGES to make a huge batch of marmalade. Music on, drink in hand, I spent a long winter evening slicing, de-pipping and prepping my way through the bottomless crate of fruit, but when my pan was full, I still had quite a few oranges left. On a whim, I sliced them up and put them into a jar with a few bay leaves and star anise, topped it up with vodka and left it to infuse for a few months. Every now and then out of curiosity I'd open the lid and the smell was just extraordinary. Bitter, fragrant, reminiscent of Campari, vermouth and Aperol, but fresher and complex, with a lovely colour.

Finally, on a beautiful summer's day, we cracked open the jar, ladled it into glasses and drank it over ice with tonic and a few sprigs of mint. It was epic, so crisp and balanced, sweet and bitter, just perfect. And while I'm still making my way through that first batch of marmalade (sorry to everyone who's had a jar as a Christmas present), I continue to make this drink every year. This recipe can be used for any fruit, and the technique is how you make sloe gin, damson vodka, quince etc. (*Pictured overleaf.*)

FOR A 2.5 LITRE KILNER JAR

10 Seville oranges, cleaned and thinly sliced

5 star anise

3 bay leaves

2 x 1 litre bottles of vodka or gin (it's worth getting something of reasonable quality)

for the sugar syrup

equal parts caster sugar and water (I usually do 300g of each)

A lot of people add sugar at the beginning of their infusions. But I prefer to add it right at the end, where you can taste as you go and have much more control. The best way to do this is by making a simple sugar syrup. This way you can ladle it into the jar bit by bit, tasting as you go to get the balance right, which always makes for a fun evening.

Place the orange slices into your Kilner jar, intermittently chucking in star anise and a bay leaf so that they're evenly spread. Pour in the vodka, right to the top, and weigh down the oranges with either a boiled stone or a fermentation weight so that they're completely submerged. Close the lid and leave for 3 months to infuse in a dark and cool place.

When the time is up, pour the vodka through a sieve into a jar. Leave the oranges in a sieve or colander with a bowl underneath, because a lot of liquid will continue to drip from them that you don't want to waste.

For the syrup, place the sugar and water in a pan on a medium heat until the sugar has completely dissolved. Leave to cool, then add a small ladleful at a time to the vodka, mixing and tasting until you find your desired balance. I think it's much better not going too sweet. So go gently, mixing well and tasting as you go . . . remembering that you can always add but never take it away. When you're happy with the flavour, either pour into a bottle or leave in the jar and seal well. Sloe gin is obviously great neat, but this orange one is fantastic over ice with a dash of tonic and some Angostura. Damson gin I find makes an incredible negroni and I even have a quince version maturing as we speak that's smelling very exciting. This is a great technique to play around with, using seasonal fruits and varying the spices: I often make these for Christmas presents.

SPRING

WHERE WINTER IS SLOW, QUIET AND CONTEMPLATIVE, spring is vivid, frantic and breathtakingly beautiful. It's where it all begins, a season of extraordinary transformation as the sharp armour of winter melts away into the honeyed haze of summer. Spring is where I am at my busiest, most inspired and frayed with all the planting, lambing and goat births coming in the space of a month. It is a season of late nights under the moon drying shivering lambs against my chest in driving rain, windowsills covered in potatoes sprouting in the soft light of March, and kid goats climbing the kitchen table in search of their next bottle. Spring is poetry, the defining season of the year, both exhausting and glorious.

I'd love to say it starts with the opening of a certain flower or the song of a bird, but for me it's always a change in the light that promises the shift into spring. It's a hopeful feeling that has been building for a while as the first pearl-white snowdrops began to appear in the shivering silver grass. Lulled by warmer days, bees emerge from months of hibernation, clearing out their hive and humming with delight in the sun. Blossom froths in the hedgerows as birds sing loudly among the thorns, territorially establishing their nesting sites by the strength of their song. The short winter grass turns an electric shade of green, skeletal trees thicken with buds and, best of all, it ends with fields full of lambs loudly calling for their mothers as kid goats skip and prance among the flowers.

I always seem to be late ordering my seeds, needing the nudge of nature to get me going. But it's such an invigorating moment. Poring over beloved websites, reading up on endless varieties and buying old favourites with a few enticing new additions. Potatoes make their way into egg-boxes on the windowsills. I put trays of chillies and tomatoes in the airing cupboard, where the heat of the boiler helps them germinate, and broad beans, peas and onions get planted outside in the damp dark soil among the worms. We use the greenhouse to get a head start on the season, using every inch for tray upon tray of beans, beetroots, turnips, courgettes and pumpkins when it would still be too cold to sow them outside. Then begins the magic, as dormant seeds awaken, bursting through the soil with leaves unfurling in search of the sun. At night, slugs slither their way through the holes of my ramshackle greenhouse to feast on the young tender seedlings. So I head out under the light of the moon and pick swathes of them in a jam jar, feeding them to the chickens in the morning (who never seem that impressed).

You wouldn't believe the colour and size of the hens' yolks at this time of year, as they feast on green shoots and fat worms that rise to the surface of the soil warmed by the sun. The supply of eggs has been pretty lean through the winter, but in spring I can hardly keep up, their nesting boxes overflowing with pale blue, green and amber-shelled eggs. Reaching in under the warm feathers of a nesting chicken I grab them by the dozen while taking sharp pecks to the hand, and walk back to the kitchen, my pockets bulging with eggs.

All this talk of hens and seeds is but a mere distraction, because all along there's only one thing on my mind in spring: lambing season. As soon as April hits, it's in the fields that I spend most of my time, stealing quick moments in the garden to build bean frames, mulch in fresh compost and continue the sowing of seeds, but in truth all I can think about are the births to come.

I've been carefully watching and feeding the girls for months through winter, with teeth bared against the bitter cold, and by now they are visibly uncomfortable with the weight of pregnancy. They walk through the fields with slow laboured steps and spend much of their time cogitating in a heap. Sheep bear pregnancy quietly, mysteriously hiding much of what they feel behind dark eyes and thick woolly coats, whereas my goats are loud in their discomfort, often wider than they are tall and huffing with deep strained breaths.

I spend my days watching with binoculars, looking for the first signs, all of us on high alert, peeking out of the windows as we walk through the house ready to race out at the faintest glimmer of an imminent birth. There are many things to look for: already swollen udders will double in size, bursting with colostrum; they rub against fence posts to align the baby within; but most obvious of all is when a mother takes herself off into a quiet corner of the field to privately begin her first contractions. Growing up in the city, I came into this with no knowledge whatsoever . . . and I have learnt

the trials and tribulations of pregnancy the hard way. Nothing prepares you for the first time you have to put your arm elbow-deep inside an animal, my phone on speaker to a neighbour taking me through the steps to turn a stuck lamb around inside the womb so that you can grab a limb to pull it out. Or, in contrast, the stark sadness of waking up to a mother pawing at her stiff cold lamb, calling quietly in desperation for it to stand. It's been a steep learning curve, one that has given me a raw appreciation for life, death and the extraordinary power of a mother's instincts. Desperately sad and distressing when things go wrong, joyful and heart-warming when they go right, but either way a deeply moving moment to behold.

More often than not, these brilliant sheep take care of themselves and all I need to do is sit quietly in the long grass and watch the strained motions unfold as a lamb enters the world, wet and shining black. The second it lands I'll race over and scoop any embryotic fluid from its mouth to make sure it can breathe, then after those first spluttering coughs, I settle back into my patch of grass and watch as the mother delicately licks her lamb clean. The cleaning takes a while, as she diligently goes over every inch of its body, nibbling at the snapped umbilical cord if still a little long. Once clean, the lamb begins trying to stand, first on to front knees and falling often. But finally, on splayed legs far too long, it wobbles on four feet like a delicate flower swaying in the wind. They need to drink within the first two hours of life, and the next stage can be painfully frustrating as the lamb teeters closer to the udders, rocked by firm licks from the mother, who always seems to turn around just as the lamb gets close. I'll watch in anguish, willing on the lamb with its fumbling steps and attempts to suckle. In extreme weather, if this is taking too long, I'll grab the mother and hold her in place, guiding the lamb towards her teats to ensure it's had a good warming drink. But generally I wait patiently, listening for those first few happy suckles, at which point my work is done for now and I can head inside.

Lambing goes on for a few weeks and I time things so that once the sheep have finished, the goats begin. By now we are in May and the miracle of spring is truly under way. The sun shimmers with a fatty warmth and the once loud birds nest quietly on speckled blue eggs, swallows dart in the vast blue skies and winter seems but a distant memory. Lambs tear around the field in mobs, skipping with delight as they chase each other's tails and worry their mothers. Kid goats obsessively try to climb anything they can find as their nannies patiently chew the cud in the hazy heat. The fields are a sea of golden buttercups and the smell of wild garlic and cherry blossom wafts through the woods, where bluebells glow in the dappled light. My washing hangs in the breeze surrounded by pink apple blossom and we can finally focus on planting out our trays of seedlings in the vegetable patch.

After the frugal months of winter, the zingy green of late May is an abundant time for us cooks. There is so much joy to be had in the food of spring as we pod baskets of fat, sugary peas and broad beans on the garden step, revelling in the cheerful snap of asparagus and puckering our lips

at the sharp pink of rhubarb swimming in a sea of custard. Every walk, I
come home with pockets overflowing with wild garlic and wood sorrel. The
weather starts getting warm enough to eat outside and much of spring is
spent with plates on our knees in the garden, munching at sandwiches with
muddy fingernails or clutching warm mugs of soup as rain clatters on the
roof of the potting shed. May is my most beloved month of the year and I
just wish it would go on forever, but the buttery warmth of summer beckons,
when we finally get to rest on our laurels and enjoy the bountiful fruits of
our frenzied labour through spring.

ASPARAGUS & SOFT-BOILED EGGS

THIS ONE'S A BIT OF A RITUAL THAT I MAKE FROM THE MINUTE THE FIRST TIPS OF asparagus arrive in spring, right to the very end of the season. It's the kind of breakfast you have on a sunny weekend. Eaten outside, listening to the radio, I can't think of much better than buttery toast and lemony asparagus dipped in the rich yolks of homegrown eggs.

Asparagus is a prime example of the joys in eating seasonally. The season is brief, only three months, and I like to make the most of it while it lasts, eating it so often that I'm almost ready for a change by the time the season is over. Then waiting patiently for another nine months, the anticipation building, never touching a spear imported from across the world; and when the first tips begin to push their way through the ground, eating it joyously again until the cycle repeats.

This is more of a way than a recipe. But let's say for three people.

SERVES 3

3 eggs

a bunch of fresh chives,
   chervil or mint

lots of butter

good bread

1 bunch of asparagus,
   woody ends removed

1 unwaxed lemon

prosciutto, or some
   smoked trout (optional)

Fill a pan large enough to hold the asparagus with water and bring it to the boil. Carefully lower in the eggs and set a timer for 6½ minutes on the dot. Now chop the herbs, get the butter out, the bread sliced and prepare for battle. A perfect breakfast is a two-man operation – get the timing wrong and you'll have cold eggs on toast that has lost its crunch.

After 3 minutes have elapsed, salt the water the eggs are in, drop in the asparagus and turn the toaster on. Action stations: when the timer goes, one person is on toast-buttering while the other is on egg-peeling. Drain the pan, peel the eggs under a running cold tap with a spoon to slide underneath the shell, but leave the asparagus in the hot dry pan with a generous knob of butter, a pinch of salt and the herbs. Toss together and leave in the pan to stay warm.

When ready, grate a touch of lemon zest over the asparagus and squeeze in a dash of juice. Place on the buttered toast with the eggs and top with yet more herbs, salt and pepper. You should have crisp toast dripping with butter, the perfect runny yolk and well-seasoned, juicy asparagus with a lovely bite.

ASPARAGUS & RICOTTA TART

THIS ZINGY TART IS MORE THAN THE SUM OF ITS PARTS, impressive but secretly very simple. It looks beautiful, tastes delicious and couldn't be easier to make – perfect as a light lunch with a sharp green salad and plate of prosciutto. Depending on what you have to hand you can really vary the herbs: wild garlic is fantastic, as are basil or dill. But in early spring, the first hardy herbs to come up in the garden are mint and chives, so I use them abundantly here. If you don't already, I'd highly recommend you grow herbs at home as, once they get going, they'll be there forever. I make these flat tarts a lot, and I love that they require no blind baking or pastry faff. You can make the pastry if you want, but usually I lean into the simplicity and go for a ready-made sheet.

SERVES 4–6

250g ricotta

50g crumbly goat's cheese (or parmesan if you prefer)

1 unwaxed lemon

a bunch of fresh mint (about 20g), leaves picked and finely chopped

a bunch of fresh chives (about 20g), finely chopped

1 sheet of puff pastry or homemade rough puff pastry (see page 310)

2 bunches of asparagus

olive oil

1 egg

Preheat your oven to 200°C fan.

Place the ricotta in a bowl with the goat's cheese and season well with salt and pepper. Grate in the zest of a whole lemon and the juice of half. Whisk together until smooth and creamy, then add most of the herbs (holding back a small handful for serving) and mix again. Have a taste and adjust the seasoning as necessary.

Roll out the puff pastry on a baking tray lined with baking parchment. With a knife, score the pastry 3–4cm from the edge all the way round; this allows the edges to rise and puff up wonderfully. Just be careful not to cut all the way through.

Snap the asparagus at the bottom to remove the woody ends – I save these over the course of a week, making the most of asparagus while it's in season, and use them to make soup. Spread the ricotta over the pastry, taking care to stay within the scored border. Then top with the spears of asparagus, drizzle with olive oil and season well. Whisk the egg and brush the edges of the pastry so they go golden in the oven. Bake for 20–30 minutes, until crisp and puffed up. When out of the oven, sprinkle with the last of the herbs and squeeze over some lemon juice. Serve immediately while piping hot.

SPRING ON A PLATE

THIS IS SO GOOD I COULD EAT IT EVERY DAY. Light, zingy, fresh and healthy, this dish is one of my late spring highlights. It's based on vignarola, an Italian classic of braised spring vegetables that usually revolves around artichokes. I find young artichokes tricky to find in Dorset, so I've gone with the things I grow and love at this time of year: peas, asparagus, broad beans, gem lettuce and herbs.

This dish involves braising; a technique of wet frying, where things are kept steamy and juicy but not so wet they get soggy. I do this with a bottle of white wine next to the pan, adding a little splash every now and then to stop things from drying out, but you can use water if you prefer. Whatever you use, the key is little splashes. Keep tasting and checking the textures as you go until each individual element is cooked to perfection. The trick to this is all in the well-timed dance of ingredients into the pan.

SERVES 4

800g broad beans, podded
  to yield about 250g

5 tbsp olive oil

1 large brown onion,
  finely diced

3 cloves of garlic,
  finely sliced

1 bunch of asparagus,
  about 250g, tips left
  whole, woody ends
  removed and stalks
  cut into chunky rounds

a bottle of white wine
  (you won't need all of it)

200g frozen peas
  (or 400g fresh peas)

1 gem lettuce,
  roughly chopped

a bunch of fresh mint
  and basil, finely chopped

2 unwaxed lemons

250g ricotta

Bring a pan of water to the boil, season it well and chuck in the broad beans. Cook for just a few minutes, then drain and immediately plunge into ice-cold water to stop them cooking further. Pinch the shells and pop out the lovely green beans.

Pour the olive oil into a wide pan, add the onion and garlic, season well with a pinch of salt and cook for 10 minutes or so, being careful not to colour the garlic, until the onion is sweet and tender. Add the asparagus with a little splash of wine. Keep stirring and cooking for a few minutes, until the asparagus is nearly but not quite tender, then add the peas. Again, season as you go and add a splash of wine here and there to keep the pan juicy. Don't overdo it, you want to keep the pan from drying out but you don't want it too wet either. Keep tasting as you go and check that the texture of the veg feels right.

The peas won't take long, so keep trying until they're ready. At this point, add the lettuce – you want it to gently collapse but still retain a nice crunch. Turn the heat off just before the lettuce is ready, as the residual heat will continue to cook things further.

Add the broad beans and most of the herbs (holding
back some for serving). Grate in the zest of one lemon, stir,
then have a taste and adjust the seasoning as necessary.

Finally, put the ricotta into a bowl and whisk well until
it becomes light and fluffy. Grate in the zest of the second
lemon, add a pinch of salt and the juice of half a lemon.
Whisk to combine, then taste to check the seasoning.

Spoon a bit of the ricotta on to each plate and spread it
slightly, then top with the warm vignarola and finish with a
drizzle of olive oil, some more herbs and a squeeze of lemon.
I like to serve this with crisp toasts rubbed with garlic, but it
is magic in an omelette or with fish or lamb.

SPINACH SOUP

SPINACH SOUP IS THE LIFEBLOOD OF MY FAMILY'S KITCHEN – cut our veins and we bleed green. At least once a fortnight we make a big batch of this vibrant elixir. Nourishing, comforting and delicious, it's perfect after a long day's work when you haven't got the energy to cook – vitality restored after a much-needed kick of iron. Great with a soft-boiled egg and crusty bread, or even with a pan-fried fillet of fish.

I must have made hundreds of bowls of this soup, yet no two have ever been the same. Sometimes a basketful of nettles or wild garlic goes in with the spinach, or cavolo nero is subbed in for an extra-green version. I often swap the potato for celeriac, use extra leeks, or make it with vegetable stock instead of chicken. Sometimes it's thick, sometimes much thinner, sometimes with crème fraîche, sometimes with Stilton. You get the idea – the possibilities are endless. You should never feel bound by a recipe, especially a soup!

SERVES 5–6

30g butter

2 tbsp olive oil

2 brown onions, finely sliced

2 leeks, finely sliced

3 large cloves of garlic,
  roughly chopped

150g potatoes,
  peeled and cubed

1 litre chicken or
  vegetable stock

600–800g spinach
  (800g gives an intensely
  green and spinachy soup;
  feel free to swap a portion
  of the spinach for cavolo
  nero, wild garlic or
  broccoli)

100g crème fraîche,
  plus extra for serving

¼ nutmeg

Place a large pan on a medium heat and melt the butter with the olive oil. Add the onions, leeks and garlic with a big pinch of salt and cook right down until sweet and tender, being careful they don't take on any colour, about 15 minutes.

Add the potatoes and the stock, then bring to a simmer and cook until the potatoes are completely tender. Add the spinach, mix it into the hot stock and cover with a lid. Cook for just a minute, the shorter the better, until the spinach has barely wilted and has gone a deep green. Immediately, either place in a blender or use an immersion blender and get it as smooth as you possibly can.

Add the crème fraîche and grate in the nutmeg, blend again, then taste for seasoning and adjust as necessary. Soups need a generous amount of salt, so keep tasting until you get it right.

Serve straight away with a dollop of crème fraîche, a drizzle of olive oil and some buttery bread. This keeps well in the fridge; just warm up the amount you need, and do it gently or you'll ruin the colour.

SPINACH, SMOKED TROUT &
CRÈME FRAÎCHE PASTA

THIS ONE'S SO GOOD THAT AFTER MAKING IT THE FIRST TIME IT BECAME AN INSTANT staple at home. It only uses one pot, takes no time at all and couldn't be easier, ideal for a simple supper right the way through the year; we make it all the time. You can use smoked salmon but personally, I've switched to trout where possible, as there are serious sustainability issues around farmed salmon and much of the wild population is on the brink of collapse.

SERVES 2

200g spinach

200g pasta (penne, but any kind of pasta works)

100g smoked trout

2–4 tbsp crème fraîche

1 unwaxed lemon

a little grated nutmeg (optional)

Bring a pan of well-seasoned water to the boil and add the spinach. Cook for no more than 20 seconds, then lift out with a pair of tongs and transfer to a colander. Chuck the pasta into the water and cook until al dente.

Meanwhile, cool the spinach under the tap, then wring out as much water as you can, either by twisting it in a tea towel or just by hand. From here there are two ways to go. You can put the spinach, trout and crème fraîche into a blender and blitz to a rough paste. Or tighten the spinach into a ball and roughly chop, then slice the trout into small pieces.

When the pasta is ready, grab a mug of the starchy water, then drain the pasta and return it to the hot pan. Add the spinach, trout and 2 tablespoons of crème fraîche, then grate in the lemon zest and season with lots of pepper. Add a splash of the pasta water and whip together to form a sauce. Keep adding more crème fraîche and pasta water until you have a nice consistency with a sauce that clings to the pasta. Squeeze in some lemon juice and season with salt (a little grated nutmeg is really good too), then mix well and taste to get the balance right. Serve immediately and dig in.

The recipe can be easily doubled or tripled, in which case the blender method is very quick and easy.

WILD GARLIC & ASPARAGUS CARBONARA

WHAT GROWS TOGETHER, GOES TOGETHER, and these two seasonal giants, asparagus and wild garlic, are especially good friends. The possibilities are endless: with eggs in the morning, in a silky risotto, puddled on to burrata, or tossed through crab and warm new potatoes. Here is a very untraditional carbonara with guanciale, asparagus, wild garlic, lemon zest and pecorino. Utter heaven, it's punchy and rich, quick to throw together and makes an excellent spring lunch after a morning birthing lambs or digging in the veg patch.

SERVES 5

250g guanciale
  or quality pancetta,
  cut into bite-size chunks
1 tbsp olive oil
500g linguine or penne
2 whole eggs and 2 yolks
30g parmesan, finely grated
40g pecorino, finely grated
2 bunches of asparagus
  (about 500g), woody ends
  snapped off, stalks sliced
  into rounds, tips left whole
about 200g wild garlic,
  finely chopped
1 unwaxed lemon

Gently fry the guanciale in a heavy-based pan with a splash of olive oil to get it going. The aim here is to let it gently caramelise in its own fat.

Get the pasta water on to a rolling boil, season well and drop in the linguine. In a bowl, whisk together the eggs, egg yolks, both cheeses and a proper whack of pepper.

When the pasta is 3 minutes from being ready, add the asparagus to the guanciale pan with a proper splash of the pasta water. Give it a toss and cook on a medium heat for 2 minutes. Add the wild garlic and give it a good stir. At this point the asparagus should be 'just' tender – you want to preserve its texture and vibrant greenness.

By now the pasta should be ready. Scoop out a couple of mugs of the starchy water, then drain the pasta and chuck it into the pot of asparagus. Take the pan off the heat. Add a little splash of pasta water to the eggs and quickly whisk through. Then add the egg mix to the pasta a little bit at a time, stirring the pasta constantly to emulsify the sauce. Once all the egg has been mixed in, add pasta water bit by bit until you find the right consistency – I use a good cup or so at least. By the end you should have a thick and glossy sauce that coats the pasta and asparagus.

Grate in the zest of the lemon, then toss the pan and taste to check your seasoning. Be careful with salt, as the guanciale and pasta water are quite salty.

Eat immediately; carbonara should never wait.

PASTA DIAVOLA WITH BURRATA & BASIL

FOR ME, THIS PASTA FITS A PERFECT SCENARIO. It's a romantic evening and you're looking to please someone special – what do you cook? You need something simple and surprising, that isn't going to have the kitchen in chaos as they arrive, no smoke, no mess, no hassle. Something impressive that you can whip up with casual flair while talking over wine and music. This is that dish: a spicy, ultra-simple tomato pasta, singing with basil and garlic, hot enough that you can feel a proper tingle. The burrata sits on top, oozing into the pasta below and providing a perfect foil to the heat. It's elegant and spicy, all important things for a night such as this.

SERVES 2
(BUT CAN BE DOUBLED)

*3 cloves of garlic,
  smashed and peeled*

3 tbsp olive oil

*1 small brown onion,
  very finely chopped*

*a pinch or two of chilli flakes
  (you want the dish spicy
  but don't overdo it)*

1 tbsp tomato purée

*1 x 400g tin of plum
  tomatoes (San Marzano
  are great)*

a few sprigs of fresh basil

20g butter

1½ tsp caster sugar

*200g pasta (casarecce or
  penne work well)*

*1 ball of burrata
  (at room temperature)*

Put the garlic cloves into a pan with the olive oil, then turn on the heat and allow the oil to slowly warm up until the garlic is sizzling. The aim here is to infuse the oil, not colour the garlic. Add the onion, chilli flakes and tomato purée and cook for 10 minutes, until the onion is tender. Cut up the tomatoes in the tin with a pair of scissors and add to the pan. Rinse out the tin with a little splash of water and pour that in too. Mix well, add a sprig of basil and bring to a gentle simmer. Leave the sauce barely bubbling for 20 minutes, until rich and thickened.

At this point, stir in the butter and sugar, then taste and adjust the seasoning as necessary. The sugar is there to balance out the acidity of the tomatoes; you want enough that it does this, without actually making it sweet.

It's now time to get the pasta on. Make sure your water is properly boiling and well seasoned, then chuck in the pasta. Keep the sauce warm while the pasta is cooking. When ready, take out a mugful of the starchy water before draining the pasta. Add the pasta to the sauce and mix well, adding generous splashes of the starchy water and a drizzle of olive oil, until it forms a silky sauce that clings to the pasta.

Spoon into deep bowls. Tear the burrata in half and place on top of the pasta. Season the burrata with salt, finish with some olive oil and a handful each of basil leaves.

CRAB & ASPARAGUS RISOTTO

CRAB AND ASPARAGUS ARE EXCELLENT FRIENDS — there's something about the delicate mix of salinity and sweetness that just works so well. Here they come together in a beautiful risotto, the crab stirred through right at the end so that it melts into the sauce with subtle touches of fennel and lemon that really bring it to life. Use the snapped woody ends of your asparagus to add extra flavour to the stock, and keep the fennel quite chunky for a welcome bit of texture. Fennel fronds or chervil would be my choice of herb here, but unless you grow them yourself (which is incredibly easy), they're hard to find, in which case I'd use a touch of dill or tarragon.

SERVES 4

1–1.5 litres fish stock
  (or vegetable stock)

300g asparagus
  (2 bunches), woody stems
  removed and reserved for
  the stock, the rest chopped
  into bite-size pieces

1 brown onion, finely diced

1 bulb of fennel, diced

100g butter

2 tbsp olive oil

3 cloves of garlic,
  finely chopped

3 tsp fennel seeds

300g risotto rice

a glass of white wine

250g white and brown
  crabmeat (about 2 picked
  crabs' worth)

1 unwaxed lemon

a bunch of fresh herbs (see
  intro), finely chopped

Throughout the entire process of making the risotto, maintaining the right heat is key – you want the pan hot enough that it's not going to take forever, but not so hot that anything sticks or burns. You need to stir constantly, so settle in and enjoy the process. Use a heavy-based pan and have the stock on a low heat next to you, with the woody asparagus stems added to infuse.

Start by gently frying the onion and fennel with 30g of the butter and a glug of olive oil. Add a generous pinch of salt and cook right down until sweet and tender, about 12–15 minutes. Add the garlic and fennel seeds, allowing them to infuse in the oil for a few minutes, then pour in the rice. Gently toast the grains for 3 minutes, stirring constantly and coating them in the oil.

Pour in the wine and cook off the alcohol before adding the first ladle of stock. When this first ladle has been absorbed, add the next. At first the stock gets absorbed quite quickly, but as time goes on it slows down. Keep repeating, stirring constantly, until the grains are nearly cooked, about 15–20 minutes.

When you feel the rice is 5 minutes away from being ready, add the asparagus and a generous pinch of salt. You're going to cook it in the risotto, so continue adding ladles of stock as above. After 5 minutes, when the asparagus is cooked but still has a nice bite, the rice should be ready. Add the crabmeat, both white and brown, and

let it warm through, mixing well so the brown meat melts into the risotto. Grate in the lemon zest and taste to check your seasoning – even though crab is from the sea, I often find it needs a good pinch of salt. Add the chervil and the remaining butter, then beat and whip it into the risotto. Add more stock if you feel it is a little dry – the risotto should be quite wet, but thick and saucy.

Taste to check your seasoning one final time and serve with a drizzle of olive oil and a squeeze of lemon.

POTATO LATKES, SMOKED TROUT,
HORSERADISH & WATERCRESS

IF YOU HAVE TIME ON A SLOW SUNDAY MORNING, this is one of the best breakfasts you can make: crisp chewy latkes, with onion, garlic and rosemary, a properly fiery horseradish sauce and smoked fatty trout. The harmony of this dish is bliss – it's a classic for a reason and a joy to eat. I must implore you to make your own horseradish sauce, it couldn't be easier and the difference is monumental. If you ever need a favour, to apologise or express your love for someone, bring them a plate of this as breakfast in bed and consider yourself absolved.

SERVES 5

for the latkes

1.2kg Maris Piper potatoes

1 brown onion

1 whole egg and 2 yolks

*3 cloves of garlic,
   finely chopped*

*a small bunch of fresh
   rosemary, leaves stripped
   and finely chopped*

40g butter, melted

olive oil, for frying

for serving

*homemade horseradish
   sauce (see page 308)*

2 bunches of watercress

*a little lemon juice and
   olive oil, for dressing*

*generous amounts of quality
   smoked trout*

Start by making the horseradish sauce following the recipe on page 308. Now move on to the latkes. Peel the potatoes and skin the onion, then grate on the coarse side of a box grater into the centre of a large clean tea towel. Twist and twist the tea towel over the sink, squeezing as much water from the potato and onion as possible. Transfer to a colander and season generously with salt. Leave for about 10 minutes so the salt has a chance to draw even more water out of the potato, then give it one last squeeze and transfer to a large bowl. Add the egg, yolks, garlic, rosemary and melted butter, season with pepper, and mix well until combined.

Place a large non-stick frying pan on a medium heat with a drizzle of olive oil. When the oil is hot, add 3 or 4 dollops of the potato mixture, gently press into shape and fry in batches until they are wonderfully golden, roughly 10 minutes per side.

Dress the watercress with a little lemon juice, olive oil and sea salt and serve with the crispy latkes, horseradish and thickly cut smoked trout.

CRISPY FISH BAPS WITH MINTED PEAS & TARTARE SAUCE

SOFT FLUFFY BUNS, CRISP FLAKING FISH, BUTTERY PEAS and a punchy tartare sauce . . . what's not to love. This is the grown-up fish finger sandwich of our childhood, an utter joy to eat and rich with nostalgia. There's no trick to it really, just seek out buns that are so fluffy your fingers leave an impression, keep the tartare sauce quite chunky and fill them to the brim with sweet buttery peas. I think Dover or lemon sole work best, but if using a slightly thicker fish, turn the frying heat to 170°C and let the breadcrumbs brown a little more slowly, by which point the fish should be cooked within. For the tartare sauce, I like to keep a lot of texture in the capers and gherkins. Dill is my preference, but lots of herbs work well here: fennel fronds, tarragon, chervil, sorrel and parsley.

SERVES 4

400g frozen peas

40g butter

1 unwaxed lemon

a bunch of fresh mint, leaves picked and finely chopped

150g plain flour

2 eggs

150g panko breadcrumbs

4 fillets of white fish

enough sunflower oil for shallow frying

4 baps

for the tartare sauce

250g natural yoghurt or homemade mayo (see page 307), I love a mix of half of each

80g cornichons, coarsely chopped

50g capers, coarsely chopped

1 shallot, finely diced

a bunch of fresh dill (20g), finely chopped

Bring a pan of salted water to the boil and drop in the peas. Keep trying one or two until you think they're ready (about 4 minutes), then drain. Give the sieve a good jiggle to get rid of as much water as possible, then return the peas to the pan and add the butter. Off the heat, crush the peas using a potato masher (or blitz in a food processor), grate in the zest of the lemon and stir in the mint. Season with salt and pepper and adjust as necessary – they will be crying out for some lemon juice, but don't add it now or the acidity will turn the peas a browny-green. But don't forget to add the lemon juice just before serving.

For the tartare sauce, simply mix the ingredients together in a bowl and have a taste. Cornichons and capers vary massively in size and strength; give them a little rinse first, as sometimes the vinegar can be way too strong. But with the tartare sauce, feel free to adjust the quantities to your taste, adding more cornichons, lemon or herbs, or yoghurt to mellow it out, just being careful not to make it overly acidic.

Set out three plates or wide, shallow bowls: one for the flour, one for the eggs and one for the panko. Season the flour with a good pinch of salt and whisk the eggs together.

CONTINUED OVERLEAF

Working with one piece of fish at a time, coat each fillet with flour, shake off any excess, then transfer it to the egg and turn to coat each side. Let any excess drip off, then transfer to the panko and turn a few times until well coated – I find pressing the fillet into the breadcrumbs really helps. Transfer to a tray and repeat with the remaining fillets.

Pour a generous glug of sunflower oil into a wide high-sided frying pan and place on a medium heat. The ideal frying temperature is between 170°C and 180°C, so use a thermometer if you have one, or test with a little pinch of panko – the panko should sizzle as soon as it hits the oil and gently turn golden. If it doesn't sizzle, the oil isn't hot enough; if it browns too quickly, the oil is way too hot. You need a good finger or two's worth of oil.

When you're ready to fry, gently place the fillets in the oil – you can do them either in batches or all at once. Fry until the first side is golden, then gently flip to cook the other side. This should take only a few minutes; if using a thicker piece of fish, cook at a lower heat initially, then turn up to brown the panko towards the end. Remove from the oil and transfer to a tray lined with kitchen paper to soak up excess oil, then sprinkle with flaky salt and a nice hit of black pepper.

As the fish fries, split the baps and lightly toast or grill. Dollop a generous amount of tartare sauce on to the base of each bap, followed by the crispy fish, then generously spoon over the peas and finish with another layer of tartare and the other half of the bap. Nostalgic bliss awaits.

MUSSELS, LEEKS, BACON & CIDER

I HAVE SUCH FOND MEMORIES PICKING MUSSELS off the rocks in Scotland at low tide and cooking vast cauldrons on the beach over a driftwood fire, flames licking up the side of the blackened pot, the lid pattering away, bursting with steam. When we got home, we'd relive those holiday memories, pulling off the beards in the sink, tapping the open mussels to make sure they closed, and juggling hot baguettes straight from the oven to the table. I must admit, I don't think at the time I loved the mussels, but oh boy did I love dunking warm bread in that sauce.

Nowadays, it's not just the sauce that I love, and moules marinière has become a recipe that I particularly enjoy playing around with, adding 'nduja or smoked haddock, using vermouth instead of wine, clams instead of mussels . . . and this little number with dry cider, smoky bacon and freshly dug leeks is particularly special. (*Pictured overleaf.*)

SERVES 2–3

200g smoked streaky bacon,
* roughly chopped*

1 tbsp olive oil

3 cloves of garlic,
* finely sliced*

1 tsp fennel seeds (optional)

400g leeks, finely chopped

1kg mussels

a large glass of dry cider

150ml double cream

a proper handful of finely
* chopped fresh parsley*

warm baguettes,
* for serving*

In a large pan, fry the bacon with a little olive oil to render out the fat, then chuck in the garlic and the fennel seeds, if using. Let them gently infuse for a few minutes, then add the leeks. Season well with a generous pinch of salt and cook the leeks right down until they are sweet and tender. You don't want any colour, so add a splash of water or two if needed to stop them catching.

While the leeks are cooking, keeping half an eye on the pan, you can prep the mussels. I pour them into a basin and submerge them in cold water with a generous handful of salt. This cleans any grit off the shells and refreshes the mussels. Then, with a big bowl next to me, I'll sift through the mussels one by one, pulling off the beard (I often use a small pair of pliers to save my fingers when cooking a big pot) and giving any open mussels a tap to make sure they close.

The idea is that the mussel keeps its shell closed when it's alive, and when cooked, the shell opens, revealing the lovely meat within. So if an uncooked mussel doesn't close with a tap, it's to be avoided. If they don't open once they're cooked, avoid those too. It's also worth noting that just because a shell is broken, it doesn't mean the mussel is bad.

CONTINUED OVERLEAF

From here it's fast and snappy. Make sure the pan is hot, pour the cider into the leeks and get it steaming, then chuck in the mussels and put the lid on. Give the pan a little shimmy and don't touch the lid for 2 minutes. Then take the lid off and turn the mussels with a spoon, as the ones at the bottom will have cooked faster than those at the top. Get the lid back on for a minute or two more, but essentially, the minute the shells open they're cooked and you want to get the pan off the heat. Pour in the cream, chuck in the parsley, crack in a good amount of pepper and season with salt. Give the pot a big mix to immerse those flavours and serve piping hot in deep bowls with lots of sauce, warm baguettes and cold cider. *HEAVEN!*

BAKED FISH WITH HERBS, LEMON & ASPARAGUS

THIS IS SUCH A GREAT WAY OF COOKING FISH – I love it. Fish can be tricky to get right, but this method of wrapping it in baking parchment is very useful and forgiving. The paper protects it from the harshness of the oven, cooking it slowly and gently, resulting in wonderfully flaky fish swimming in its own sauce among the veg below. You can play around with the veg here, and it's a method that can be used throughout the seasons.

Fish spend their life in very cold conditions compared to us mammals. Therefore, compared to meat, fish needs to reach a much lower temperature to be cooked. The greatest trick I was taught is to take a skewer (or knife) and poke it into the centre of your fish while it's cooking, leave it for a few seconds, then bring it out and touch it to your lip. If it's warm, your fish is cooked, if it's hot, you've gone too far. You can use any fresh white fish for this – plaice, pollack, sole, monkfish, cod, turbot and hake are all fantastic – just ask your fishmonger what's best that day.

SERVES 4

200g baby courgettes

a large bunch of asparagus, about 250g, woody ends removed

100g frozen peas

3 tbsp olive oil

1 large fillet or 4 small fillets of fresh white fish

40g butter, thinly sliced

1 unwaxed lemon, thinly sliced

a small glass of dry white wine

for serving

buttery Jersey Royals (or any new potatoes)

fresh herbs – wild garlic or chives, dill, chervil, fennel fronds, mint, etc.

Preheat your oven to 180°C fan.

Slice the courgettes into rounds the thickness of your little finger. Do the same with the stalks of the asparagus but leave the tips whole.

Line a baking tray with foil and then with baking parchment, making sure they both go up the sides. Chuck in the courgettes, asparagus and peas, drizzle over the olive oil and season well with salt, then give the tray a shake and toss. Bake for 15 minutes, until the veg is sizzling. Take the tray out and top with the fish. Season the fish with salt and pepper, then top with the butter and lemon slices. Pour in a generous splash of dry white wine, fold over the parchment and place back in the oven for 15–20 minutes, until the fish is just cooked.

Take the tray out, drizzle with olive oil and spoon some of the winey buttery sauce over the fish and veg. Serve with new potatoes drowned in butter and top with a generous amount of fresh herbs. Wild garlic or chives are a favourite here, but dill, chervil, fennel fronds and mint are great too. This is lovely with a lemony mayo on the side.

CHICKEN ROASTED OVER LEMON, FENNEL & POTATO

THERE IS A MAGICAL THING THAT HAPPENS WHEN YOU ROAST A CHICKEN above a tray of seasonal veg. The skin crisps and bubbles as the fat and juices drip down on to the veg below, which suck up all that flavour and take on an almost gooey and caramelised texture. Here it's a tray of fennel, new potatoes and lemon, with bay and a head of garlic too, one of those dishes we make again and again at home. As they cook, the fennel and lemon flavour the chicken from below and the steam released keeps it wonderfully juicy. Minimal work, only uses one tray and makes its own sauce – as roast chickens go, this is one to write home about. Serve simply with a sharp green salad and aïoli or romesco…a Sunday lunch fit for a king.

SERVES 5

1 organic chicken
olive oil
800g new potatoes
a whole head of garlic
1 unwaxed lemon
3 bulbs of fennel
5 bay leaves
a glass of dry white wine
a knob of butter (optional)

for serving
aïoli (see page 307)
  or romesco sauce
  (see page 192)
green salad

I like to spatchcock my chicken, but if you want to roast it whole, just add another 20 minutes or so to the cooking time. To spatchcock a chicken, using a sharp pair of shears, just cut all the way along one side of the spine, then turn it over, open out the chicken and crush to flatten. Your butcher will be happy to do this for you. Now rub the chicken generously with olive oil and season liberally all over with salt. Leave it on the counter for an hour so the salt can penetrate and the chicken loses the chill of the fridge.

Preheat your oven to 240°C fan.

While the chicken is coming up to temperature, crack on with the veg. Cut the potatoes into halves or quarters depending on their size, and smash the head of garlic to release the individual cloves, then give each a bash just to lightly break them. Cut the lemon into quarters and then into 1cm slices, and roughly slice the fennel lengthways. Put all the veg, bay leaves and lemon into a large deep baking tray, but don't stack it too high or it'll cook unevenly. Then drizzle over a generous amount of olive oil, season well with salt and give the pan a good shake so the salt and olive oil cover everything evenly.

Place the chicken on top, then whack the tray into the oven and cook for 20–30 minutes at this high temperature

CONTINUED OVERLEAF

until the skin takes on a lovely bit of colour. Then pour in the white wine, let a bit of heat out of the oven and turn the heat right down to 140°C fan. Cook for another 20 minutes or so, until the chicken is about 66°C at its thickest point, or until the juices run clear. Remove the chicken from the oven, turn the heat to 180°C fan, give the veg a good mix and leave to carry on cooking until they're ready, adding a splash more wine, even a knob or two of butter if they're looking a little dry. Leave the chicken resting on a large plate to catch the juices with a sheet of foil loosely on top; this rest allows it to fully cook through and reabsorb its juices.

After 10–15 minutes you should have a well-rested chicken and beautifully cooked veg. Pour any juices that have dripped from the chicken into the veg, place the chicken on top and carve directly into the tray. Serve with lots of the veg, and hopefully a bit of the cooking liquor still at the bottom of the tray. I like a generous dollop of aïoli or romesco, or both, and one of my favourite things is the salad at the end, mixed through the veg and chicken gravy with a dash of lemon and olive oil.

BRAISED SAUSAGE, FENNEL & TOMATO STEW
with wet polenta

I LOVE MAKING BRAISED SAUSAGE STEWS. This punchy number with tomato, olive and fennel is the perfect warming lunch after a frosty spring morning. Lambs are calling in the fields, kid goats need bottle-feeding and there's hours of mulching to do in the veg patch. What could be better than a hearty tomato stew inspired by puttanesca, with the warming hum of chilli and salty twang of Kalamata olives. The sausages and fennel get cooked in the sauce, absorbing so much flavour and becoming wonderfully tender. I like to serve this on a bed of wet buttery polenta, eaten piping hot by the fire in deep bowls. But it goes equally well with rice, potatoes, even tossed through pasta. (*Pictured overleaf.*)

SERVES 5–6

10–12 quality chipolata sausages (or larger sausages if you prefer)

a splash of red wine

5 cloves of garlic, smashed and roughly chopped

5 anchovies

2 tsp fennel seeds

a generous pinch of chilli flakes

2 large red onions, finely sliced

2–3 bulbs of fennel, depending on size, sliced

a few bay leaves

2 x 400g tins of plum tomatoes

1 jar of pitted Kalamata olives, 160g drained weight

for serving

finely chopped fresh parsley

olive oil

Start by frying the sausages in a heavy-based pan. The aim here is to quickly caramelise them but not cook them through. Once they've taken on some colour, remove from the pan and set to one side. Turn the heat right down and add a splash of wine to deglaze the pan. Then add the garlic, anchovies, fennel seeds and chilli flakes and let them gently infuse in the fat that has rendered from the sausages. Be very careful they don't burn or take on any colour. After a few minutes, when the anchovies have melted, add the onions with a generous pinch of salt and cook for 10–15 minutes, until sweet and tender, adding a splash of water if they begin to stick or catch.

Once the onions are soft and sweet, add the fennel, bay leaves and tomatoes. Rinse out the tins with a splash of water and pour that tomatoey water into the pan. Season well with a pinch of salt and a few turns of pepper, then put the lid on and gently simmer for 1 hour, stirring every so often, until the fennel is tender and the sauce has thickened.

When the fennel is tender, add the sausages and olives, give it all a good mix and cook for a further 5–10 minutes with the lid off so the flavours can get to know one another. If you are using fatter sausages, they might need a little longer to ensure they are cooked through. Have a final taste to check the seasoning.

CONTINUED OVERLEAF

FOR THE WET POLENTA

SERVES 5-6

750ml water (or whole
milk), plus more as needed

150g coarse polenta

50g unsalted butter

40g parmesan (or Gruyère)

Generally, your polenta will have the rough quantity of water to polenta given on the back of the packet, so do only use this as a guide. I prefer coarse polenta, as I find it much more interesting in texture and flavour, but it takes longer to cook and needs a lot of stirring, so use a faster version if you don't have time for the faff.

Start by bringing the water up to a boil in a pan (you can also use milk for a richer version), then turn down the heat until it's barely bubbling and season well with salt. Slowly pour in the polenta in a gentle stream (I use a jug for this), whisking continuously to prevent lumps. It will begin to thicken and bubble like lava – turn the heat right down so it is barely bubbling at all, and stir relatively constantly for the next 30 minutes.

When the polenta grains are tender, have a taste to check this, adding more water (or milk) to find the consistency you like. You're not looking for it to be pourable, but you do want it quite loose. Chuck in a serious knob of butter and grate in a generous amount of parmesan (Gruyère is also amazing). A little pepper is nice too. Stir, taste and check the consistency as it will thicken on the plate. Serve in deep bowls by the ladleful and top with the sausage stew and lots of sauce. Finish with a smattering of parsley and a drizzle of olive oil. One of my favourite recipes in the book, I'd move mountains for a bowl of this.

BAVETTE STEAK, ANCHOVY CREMA & RADISHES

THE STAR OF THE SHOW HERE IS THE ANCHOVY CREMA, which is my go-to sauce, a secret weapon of sorts. It's silky, umami-rich and voluptuous, essentially a velvety mayo thickened with bread and using boiled eggs instead of raw, which gives the texture real substance. It's great with slow-cooked lamb; perfect alongside a crispy chicken thigh; but also simply with crisp radishes on toast on a cold spring morning. A particular favourite is to make a warm salad of potatoes, radishes, peas, gem lettuce, asparagus, broad beans and peas, tossed with lemon, butter and chives, then pour this on to a deep puddle of anchovy crema so you can dip and dunk to your heart's content. Here it's served alongside a juicy steak with boiled potatoes and radishes, which is delicious, though just a suggestion.

You need a fast blender for this, and add the oil incredibly slowly so it doesn't split, then taste and taste to perfect the seasoning. It will happily keep for a week in the fridge, but mine's always finished long before that.

SERVES 4

for the anchovy crema

2 eggs

*40g fresh sourdough
 (no crust)*

*1 tin of salted anchovies,
 about 10 fillets*

1 clove of garlic

½ tablespoon Dijon mustard

1 lemon

200ml sunflower oil

60ml cold water

CONT. OVERLEAF

First make the anchovy crema. Soft-boil the eggs for 6½ minutes, then plunge into cold water and peel. Quarter the eggs, then place in a high-speed blender.

Tear in the sourdough, add the anchovies with their oil, the garlic, mustard, the juice of half the lemon (save the rest for later) and a pinch of salt. Blitz this to a very smooth paste, then with the blender running, start trickling in the oil incredibly slowly so that it doesn't split. Use tiny splashes of cold water if you find it is not mixing well enough. Keep going until all the oil is used up. Then add the water bit by bit while blending to find your desired consistency. Taste to check the seasoning, adding a touch more salt and lemon juice if need be. It should be intense, smooth and very moreish. Store in a jar in the fridge if not using straight away.

Remove the steak from the fridge, season generously with salt on both sides and leave to come up to room temperature. Scrub the potatoes and place in a pan with cold water, season well and add a sprig of mint if you have one to hand. Bring up to a gentle simmer and cook until tender. Meanwhile, get a frying pan fiercely hot, drizzle a little olive oil over the steaks, then place in the pan.

CONTINUED OVERLEAF

4 bavette steaks,
    or 1 or 2 large ones
400g Jersey Royals
    (or any new potatoes)
a sprig of fresh mint
    (optional)
1 tbsp olive oil
100g unsalted butter
1 clove of garlic, smashed
a sprig of fresh thyme
a bunch of fresh chives,
    finely chopped
a handful of radishes

Press each steak into the pan and then just let it do its thing, don't be tempted to move it. The aim is to quickly caramelise it on one side, then flip and do the same on the other. This should only take 2–3 minutes a side. Then turn the heat right down and add roughly a third of the butter, the smashed clove of garlic and a sprig of thyme. Let the butter foam, tilt the pan and baste over the steaks. Remove when they feel medium rare and leave to rest on a plate for 5 minutes with the cooking juices. The thickness of your steak completely determines how long this will take. If you have a temperature probe, the inside temperature should be around 50–55°C.

Drain the potatoes, chuck in the rest of the butter, season and add the chives (holding back some for serving). Stir to break up the potatoes a little so they absorb the butter. To serve, spoon a generous amount of anchovy crema on to the plate, slice the rested steak and place on top, then finish with the potatoes and radishes. Spoon over any browned butter from the pan and finish with yet more chives and pepper.

HAM HOCK, PEA & MINT STEW

IN THE COLDER MONTHS THERE ARE FEW THINGS MORE NOURISHING than a steaming bowl of broth and after a long day in the bitter wind when the cold has sunk deep into my bones, there is nothing I'd rather come home to. A smoked ham hock produces one of the finest broths there is, it's old-school cooking at its finest, using a cheaper, tougher cut of meat that slowly simmers away to create an unctuous and lip-smacking stew. A good smoked ham hock can take some tracking down (I get mine online), but the effort you go to in finding one will be beyond worth it.

The ham hock does need a bit of time to slow cook, at least 4 hours, but this can be done the day before. Just leave the hock in its broth, ready to finish the stew the next day. Any leftover broth makes a particularly fine pea soup with parmesan and roasted garlic.

SERVES 6

to poach the ham hock

1 smoked ham hock, 1.5kg

1 leek

3 carrots

2 brown onions

3 bay leaves

a parmesan rind

a few peppercorns

for the stew

3 tbsp olive oil

2 large brown onions,
  finely chopped

5 cloves of garlic, smashed

2 leeks, roughly chopped

4 carrots, roughly chopped

3 bay leaves

CONT. OVERLEAF

To start, place the ham hock, vegetables, bay leaves and parmesan rind in a large pot (one big enough to take the vegetables too). This early stage is a great way of clearing out the fridge – any leek tops, scraggy looking bits of garlic, bacon rinds or dried herbs and parsley stalks can all go in. Top up with water so that everything is submerged, and add a handful of peppercorns and a generous pinch of salt. Bring up to the gentlest of simmers, skimming off any foam and leave to bubble slowly for 4–5 hours, until the hock is falling off the bone. At this stage you can either leave the ham in its broth to cool until the next day, or crack on right away.

Remove the hock and set to one side until it's cool enough to handle. Then strip the meat from the bone, making sure to get every bit of fat and skin off, as these are gold dust to the stew. It should fall apart and be ludicrously tender. I would do this by hand and break the pieces into bite-size chunks. Keep the meat in a bowl, submerged in a ladle or two of the broth. Now strain the rest of the broth; the aim here is just to remove the used-up veg. All that shimmering fat is essential, as it lends the broth its wonderfully unctuous quality.

CONTINUED OVERLEAF

a glass of white wine or cider

800g potatoes, roughly chopped

200g pearl barley (optional)

400g frozen peas

a generous bunch of fresh mint leaves and parsley, finely chopped

crusty bread and butter, for serving

Heat the olive oil in a large, heavy-based pan and add the onions. Fry gently until tender but not browned, about 10 minutes. Add the smashed garlic cloves, fry for a few minutes to infuse the oil, then add the leeks, carrots and bay leaves. Cook this for 5 minutes just to let the flavours of the veg come together, then pour in the white wine and cook until the alcohol evaporates.

Add the potatoes and the pearl barley, if using, then pour in enough broth so that everything is submerged and cook for 30 minutes or more, until the potatoes (and pearl barley) are tender. Put the ham hock back in, add the peas and top up with more broth if it needs it – you want this properly soupy. Warm the hock through, tasting and adjusting the seasoning as necessary. Try a couple of peas to make sure they're cooked. Remember this is a lot of liquid, and it may need a pretty generous amount of salt. Add the herbs and serve the broth in deep bowls, with crusty bread healthily slathered in butter.

LAMB STEW WITH PEARL BARLEY
& WILD GARLIC

THERE'S A DAY I LOOK FORWARD TO EACH YEAR when the mood of winter shifts to spring. It's a change you can feel in the air, a joyousness, a bounce to life. After months of impenetrable cloud and unrelenting rain, the sun breaks through and the grey, lifeless light of winter begins to reawaken with the fizz and energy of spring. The goats lie basking in the sun, birds sing louder and wild daffodils emerge in the woods. The beehives hum with life and perhaps most excitingly of all, spears of wild garlic and other wild delights begin to burst through the banks and hedgerows.

This comes from one of those days when, walking home from the woods with a handful of young wild garlic, I was cold and desperate for something properly nourishing. So here we have a brothy and unctuous stew of meltingly tender lamb, packed with veg and herbs and underpinned by the soothing texture of pearl barley. While the wild garlic is fantastic, I appreciate it can be hard to find; have no fear, as this is equally delicious with cavolo nero or even just a handful of parsley. (*Pictured overleaf.*)

SERVES 6

750g lamb neck fillet (or thick-cut lamb shoulder)

3 tbsp olive oil

5 cloves of garlic, roughly chopped

3 brown onions, finely diced

5 salted anchovies

a large glass of red wine

3 bay leaves

a few sprigs of fresh thyme

4 carrots, cut into jaunty chunks

4 celery sticks, thinly sliced

1.2 litres chicken stock (see page 306)

200g pearl barley

300g wild garlic (or cavolo nero), roughly chopped

apple cider or sherry vinegar, to finish

Start by preparing the lamb neck. Cut it in half lengthways, then slice across for thick chunks. Season the pieces generously with salt, then leave to one side for 15 minutes so the salt can penetrate while you prep the veg.

When ready, pour the olive oil into a deep heavy-based pan and place on a medium heat. Once the oil is hot, chuck in the lamb – the aim here is to properly caramelise the meat all over, which adds so much flavour to the stew. When it's good and brown, remove and set to one side.

Turn the heat down and add the garlic, onions and anchovies with a generous pinch of salt and cook for 10 minutes, until sweet and sticky. Pour in the wine and reduce by half, then add the bay leaves, thyme, carrots and celery. Cook the veg for another 10 minutes, then put the lamb back in, pour over the stock, put the lid on and gently simmer at the faintest of bubbles for 30 minutes.

At this point have a taste and adjust the seasoning as necessary – I'm sure a good whack of pepper will do it good. Add the pearl barley, give it a stir, then put the lid

CONTINUED OVERLEAF

back on and gently simmer for another 30–45 minutes, until the pearl barley is cooked. At this point, the lamb should be meltingly tender. Add the wild garlic, give it a good stir and let it briefly wilt. Pour in the tiniest splash of vinegar, being careful not to overdo it, the aim here just being to brighten up the stew, not make it taste vinegary. Stir and taste to check your seasoning for a final time.

Serve piping hot in deep bowls, with a drizzle of good olive oil.

RHUBARB & CUSTARD TARTLETS

RHUBARB AND CUSTARD, WHAT CAN I SAY, THE PERFECT EXAMPLE of two ingredients that bring out the best in each other. The way the custard exaggerates the vibrant pop of sharpness in the rhubarb here is just divine. These tarts are also deceptively easy to make, and it's a recipe I use year-round with all sorts of fruit throughout the seasons. Raspberries are unbelievably good, as are thinly sliced apples, apricots, wild plums and pears. The recipe makes quite a big batch of custard, which keeps in the fridge for a good few days and can be used in many sweet adventures.

SERVES 6

1 vanilla pod
500ml whole milk
125g caster sugar
5 egg yolks
40g cornflour
1 sheet of puff pastry,
  or homemade rough puff
  pastry (see page 310)
1kg rhubarb
apricot jam, for glazing
demerara sugar,
  for sprinkling

Start by making the custard. Carefully cut the vanilla pod in half, scrape out the seeds and place in a saucepan with the milk, the empty vanilla pod and half the caster sugar. Put the pan on a low heat and warm through until the vanilla infuses and the sugar melts, being careful not to scald the milk.

In a separate bowl, whisk the egg yolks with the rest of the caster sugar until they go pale and fluffy, then add the cornflour and mix through.

Remove the vanilla pod from the milk, then pour the hot milk little by little on to the egg yolks, whisking constantly. This tempers the yolks, which gets them used to the heat ahead of cooking. When you have mixed in all the milk, pour the mixture back into the pan and place on a low heat. You need to slowly warm up the custard while constantly whisking and scraping the bottom of the pan until it thickens enough to really coat the back of a spoon. I use a spatula and make sure that no part of it stays on the bottom of the pan for too long, otherwise the egg can overcook and go lumpy. The custard should be wonderfully thick and wobbly, but do not overcook it and do not rush. The minute it thickens, take off the heat and immediately push it through a sieve into a bowl to cool.

CONTINUED OVERLEAF

If not using the custard straight away, scatter a small amount of icing sugar over the surface to act as a buffer, then press a sheet of baking parchment or cling film on to the surface so that it doesn't form a skin in the fridge.
You can make this in advance.

Preheat your oven to 200°C fan.

Roll the puff pastry out on a baking tray lined with baking parchment. You can either make one big tart or individual ones, so cut the sheet of puff as you wish – I usually cut it into six sections. Carefully score the edges of the pastry, leaving a 2cm border round the edge. Be careful not to go right through the pastry, but make sure your incisions are deep enough and connect with each other; this lets the edges of the pastry rise.

Take a few spoons of the custard and spread generously over the inner square of pastry, being careful not to go over the scored borders. I like to add about a finger's depth of custard. Cut the rhubarb into lengths and place on top of the custard, nestling them in a little. You want to cram on as much rhubarb as possible. You can make the tarts up to this stage, then chill in the fridge for up to 24 hours until ready to bake.

Warm the apricot jam in a pan with a tiny splash of water until you have a paintable mixture, then with a pastry brush, paint the rhubarb and the edges of the pastry. This will ensure the pastry has a lovely sheen and helps it go golden brown. Bake for about 20 minutes, or until the pastry has picked up some nice colour and the rhubarb is cooked.

Remove from the oven and sprinkle with a little demerara sugar. Leave to cool for a few minutes, but definitely tuck in while still warm.

COFFEE SEMIFREDDO WITH SALTED CARAMEL PISTACHIOS

THIS IS AN ABSOLUTE SHOWSTOPPER OF A DISH. Semifreddo is a genius Italian no-churn ice cream that requires no making of custard or snazzy equipment – you just whisk together a silky mousse and freeze it. It has the most pleasing texture, somewhere between marshmallow and nougat, that gets even better as it melts. This one is rich with coffee and vanilla, and studded with these utterly addictive salted caramel pistachios. It might seem like a complex recipe at first glance, and you do need to make a caramel, but these things are easier than they seem and I will show you the way. Once you've got the hang of it you'll be able to play around with the base recipe and make your own versions. Try different nuts, shaving in dark chocolate or ditching the coffee and nuts altogether and folding in a sour cherry compote or other stewed fruit. (*Pictured overleaf.*)

SERVES 8–10

for the caramelised
pistachios

*100g pistachios
(ideally with the
skins removed)*

100g caster sugar

a good pinch of flaky salt

for the semifreddo

5 egg whites

200g caster sugar

1 vanilla pod

300ml double cream

*30ml cold, strong espresso
(or some really strong,
thick coffee)*

Preheat your oven to 180°C fan and line a baking tray with a silicone mat or baking parchment. Toast the pistachios for about 10 minutes, until crisp and crunchy. They burn easily, so set a timer.

While the nuts are toasting, pour the 100g of sugar into a wide pan, ideally a silver-coloured pan so you can see the colour of the caramel as it changes. Shake the sugar about so it spreads evenly and place the pan on a medium-high heat. The sugar will begin to melt at the edges and then spread inwards – it's tempting to give it a stir and help it melt evenly, but don't, or it will crystallise. You can give the pan a shimmy and a shake, just no stirring. Watch the colour: at first it will be translucent, then it will begin to caramelise and darken. You're looking for a reddish colour.

When the caramel is ready, turn off the heat and pour in the nuts while they're still hot. Having the nuts hot gives you time to stir them through the caramel without it setting too quickly. Add a generous pinch of flaky salt and mix with a spatula to completely coat them in the caramel, then quickly pour on to the lined tray and leave to cool. When set, bash with a rolling pin to break apart the caramelised

CONTINUED OVERLEAF

nuts – don't turn them to dust, but you don't want the chunks too big either. Instead of great big clumps, you're looking for individual nuts and halves.

From here, the hard work is done and it's plain sailing. Grab a terrine dish or bread tin, roughly 25cm x 10cm, and line it with two or three sheets of cling film – this is vital in getting the semifreddo out later on. Whisk the egg whites in a scrupulously clean bowl until they form stiff peaks. I like to do this by hand with a balloon whisk. The thing with egg whites is that you can overwhisk them, where they go so stiff that they're actually quite hard and almost brittle, which makes the foam tricky to stir through the cream and leaves clumps. You are looking for a silky foaminess that still has movement; if you lift up your whisk it should leave a spike that folds over itself, not a stiff foam that has gone too hard. If you're using a machine, keep a very clear eye on it and the minute the eggs form a trail that leaves that curled spike, they are ready. At this stage, add the sugar little by little while whisking continuously to create a lovely and light meringue. In a separate bowl, scrape out the vanilla pod and add to the double cream, then whip until it thickens and again leaves little ribbons behind the whisk. I feel like I may have made this sound scary, but don't let this put you off, you're just whisking something, it's easy. All I'm saying is that there is a perfect texture to aim for and it's better to be under than over.

Carefully fold the pistachios and coffee into the cream, then fold the meringue into the mixture using a spatula. Do this all slowly, little by little, trying to retain as much air as possible. Pour into your prepared dish, fold over the cling film and place in the freezer until it sets. I find it takes at least 6–8 hours and is best made the night before.

To serve, simply turn the semifreddo out of the mould, peel off the cling film and slice thickly on a breadboard. Quickly wrap any leftovers back up and place in the freezer for a much-needed boost after a long day.

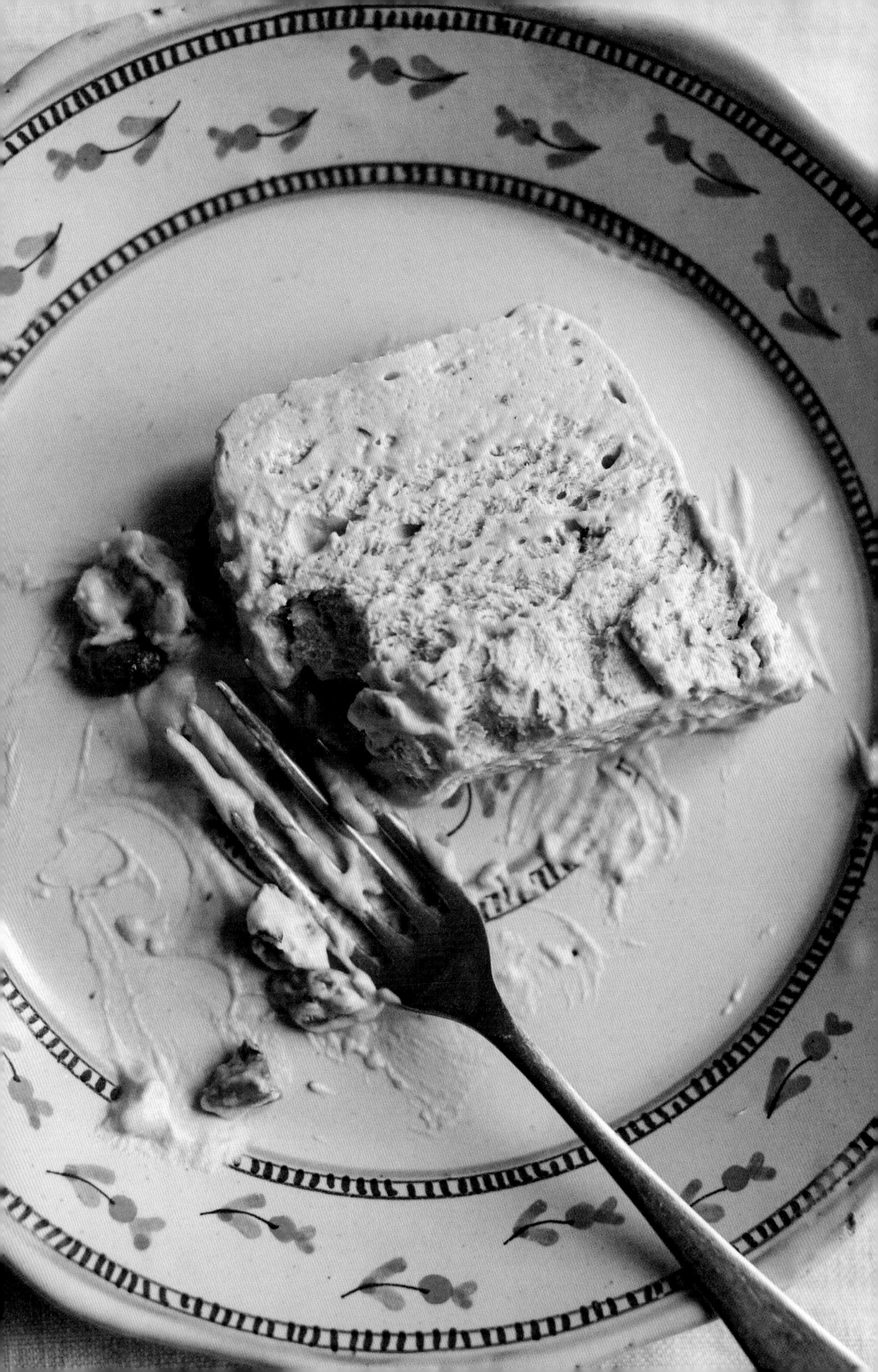

ELDERFLOWER PANNA COTTA WITH ROASTED STRAWBERRIES & BLACK PEPPER

I LOVE THE SIMPLICITY OF PANNA COTTA. When done right, light and not too sweet, it's an elegant end to a meal. I've toned down the sugar and added some buttermilk, which lends a subtly acidic edge that cuts through the richness. I've used elderflower, but chamomile flowers (either wild or from a teabag), lemon verbena and rose all work wonderfully. If you can't get your hands on any of these, you can't go wrong with good old vanilla. Usefully, this recipe can be made the day before you want to eat it.

Two important points: first, don't let the cream get too hot; you want it steaming but not bubbling to melt the sugar. Second, if you're adding any of the soft fresh leaves or flowers mentioned above, add them towards the end with the buttermilk and gelatine so that they can slowly infuse and retain their freshness. Keep smelling and tasting the cream until you get the strength you want, then pass it through a sieve. But if you're going with vanilla, spices or dried chamomile, I would add them to the cream from the start so that they release a good amount of flavour.

SERVES 6

300ml quality double cream
150ml whole milk
120g caster sugar
3 leaves of gelatine
100ml buttermilk
3–5 fresh heads of elderflower, picked in the morning sun (or 1 vanilla pod, halved and seeds scraped into the cream along with the pod to infuse)
600g strawberries, tops removed and cut in half lengthways
freshly ground black pepper
a few drops of rose water

Put the cream, milk and 80g of the caster sugar into a saucepan over a low heat. Bring up to just before a simmer, whisking as you go, until the sugar melts, then turn the heat off.

Put some cold water into a bowl, then drop in the gelatine leaves and leave for 3 minutes to soak. Lift out the gelatine, squeeze out all the water, add to the hot cream and whisk through. Add the buttermilk along with the elderflower heads, keeping a few flowers back for decoration. Stir again and leave the elderflowers to infuse – it should smell stunning.

After 5–10 minutes, have a taste to check the strength of the infusion; if you are happy, pour the mixture through a sieve into a jug. Then pour into six ramekins or dariole moulds, but don't fill them up too high; it's a rich pudding and you don't need much – I only go half or three-quarters of the way up. Place a little circle of baking parchment or cling film on top of each mould, gently pressing it into the cream. This stops a hard skin forming, which would ruin the silky texture. Place the ramekins in the fridge for at least 4 hours, until properly set.

CONTINUED OVERLEAF

Half an hour or so before serving, make the roasted strawberries. Preheat your oven to 180°C fan and line a baking tray with baking parchment. Spread the strawberries over the tray, scatter over the remaining 40g of sugar and give them a good toss so they're coated evenly. Add some freshly cracked pepper, then roast for 20 minutes. Remove from the oven and add literally just a few drops of rose water. Go carefully, as it's incredibly strong and you're just looking for a subtle undertone. Give the pan a shimmy to disperse it.

To serve, dip each panna cotta mould into boiling water for just a few seconds, then place a plate on top and flip. If it doesn't release because of the vacuum, it sometimes needs a bit of a shake – just hold the plate and mould tightly while you do so. Spoon over the warm strawberries with lots of their liquor and top with a few decorative elderflowers.

SUMMER

AFTER THE FRANTIC CHAOS OF SPRING, THE ETERNAL SLUMBER of summer begins with an eruption of elderflower in the hedgerows. Swathed in morning mist, we head up the hill to pick them by the basket and leave the heads in pots of water to infuse for cordial, skimming off the tiny pollen beetles that rise to the surface. Swallows flit across fields rippling with heat, darting among the flowers and catching flies on the wing. The June grasses are now waist deep and sticky with pollen, singing with throngs of grasshoppers that leap from the shadows with every step. Buzzards hover high in the sky, their screeching calls piercing the vast blue quiet as fat greedy lambs call for milk down below. My sheep spend most of their day lurking in the protective shade of overgrown hedges, escaping the heat in their heavy woollen coats, reminding me to nudge the shearer once again.

Clouds of flowers surround the farm and we pick cow parsley, sweet peas and buttercups by the armful, pouring them into jugs and vases to fill the house with their dizzying scent. Light dances in windows thrown open to release the cloying heat within, and sheets billow on the washing line like the lonely sails of a ship at sea. I watch a pair of kid goats chewing at the corners of a duvet, their grassy mouths leaving little stains as they collapse into a yawning puddle under the washing line. Each day starts with a good hour of watering, the sun on my shoulders with coffee in hand, moving the sprinkler around the veg patch and enjoying the pitter-patter of heavy drops against dark green leaves. I'll munch at peas and nasturtium flowers as I go, tugging at weeds and tying in beans that twist their way up hazel frames. In the wet heat of the polytunnel, things are thriving: tomatoes climb their strings among a sea of basil and the smell coming off the vines is rich and overwhelming. It's impossible to keep up with the pace of growth, and by July a jungle of spiky cucumbers hang from the ceiling and my chillies have been swallowed by a swathe of marigolds and courgettes.

One evening in July I finally get a call from the sheep shearer, who can come first thing tomorrow. We set up corrals in the small paddock and gather the sheep off the hill. I love walking them down through the fields, beckoning with our hands and yipping as a wave of woolly bodies ripples through the grass leaving corduroy streaks in its wake. Shearing is an art, and watching a master at work is a sight to behold. He holds the sheep,

carefully stretching them in different positions so their skin doesn't bunch up as sharp blades glide across bowed bodies in sweeping motions. What would take me half an hour he can do in a minute, and the sheep lie in a yoga-like trance, with one eye beadily watching the whirring razor as their wool falls away. As he finishes, I race in to tightly fold the fleeces, bundling them into bags as the sheep run off enjoying their newfound breezy lightness. There's always an amusing moment as dumbfounded lambs run from their now unrecognisable mothers, who chase them in desperation through the long summer grass. Once finished, we bask in the sun, enjoying the fruits of our labour with cups of tea in lanolin-covered hands, talking over the price of wool and the good old days when there was value in shearing sheep. Now, sadly, wool is more or less worthless, much of it destined for the compost or, even worse, burnt on the fire. Shearing these days is purely for the welfare of the sheep.

Another highlight of summer is the bee swarms. We are avid beekeepers, and Mum and I look after three hives by the veg patch that are thriving on the blossoming flowers around the house and wildflower in the meadows. I planted a huge swathe of phacelia and borage that bustles with bees all day long, and walking past the hives you can hear them roaring with life. But when the colony gets too large it splits, and half the bees eat as much honey as they can before heading off with the queen to find a new home. This year I was pottering about in the greenhouse when I heard the roar of a swarm above me. Walking out, I was engulfed by a cloud of 30,000 bees, and watched in awe as they began to settle on the chimney, which seems to be a magnet for these swarms – it's happened every year we've lived here. With an active chimney not being the best place for them to settle, Mum and I lit a small grassy fire to smoke it out in an attempt to slow the bees down while a neighbour raced over with his extra-long ladders. Donning my bee suit I climbed the house with basket and bee brush in hand to rescue the swarm. Sweating in the blue hazy heat of the endless sky above me, I sat on the roof and scooped a calm bundle of bees about the size of a watermelon into my basket. Carefully closing the lid, I passed the buzzing basket down the ladder and we left it in the shade of an oak tree so the swarm could settle. Then, in the evening, we gently poured the bees into a spare hive with a few

brood frames and some honey to get them going. We are holistic beekeepers, looking after them purely for the joy in beholding their fascinating lives, taking very little honey if at all, providing sanctuary and care in the knowledge they pollinate the land around us.

Sadly, as much as I wish it would, the passage of summer waits for no man, and as the flowers in the meadows turn to seeds and the scorched earth splits with cracks, we wait on the weather for a window to make our hay. We split the harvest with our friendly neighbours in return for their help in the form of wonderfully archaic machines and barns for storage, coming together to preserve the bountiful summer grasses to feed our animals through the leaner times of winter. With a blistering spell ahead, their mower clatters through the fields, spitting dust and dandelion seeds as buzzards and hawks watch for darting rabbits and voles. Great spinning rakes flick the cut grass into neat lines, to dry evenly under the fierce summer sun. Then, after a few days, when the hay is crisp and brittle, we

begin baling. The rusty baler trundles down the rows with its flailing arms, sucking up the grass and spitting out weighty green bales. Bolts shear and work pauses as we spend hours fixing the puzzling machine, scratching heads and drilling out rusty screws with oil-smudged hands, before the whirring arms of the machine can begin again. We stack the bales on a trailer that grows as high as a house, using every drop of sun and working late into the night until it's time to sit under the warm light of the moon with fizzing glasses of homemade cider in hand.

Waking with bruised bodies, we have a quick breakfast of broad beans, bacon and eggs, before loading the last of the bales in the cooler morning sun. Engulfed by the smell of hot hay drying in the wind, we throw the remaining few bales on the teetering tower and watch as the tractor precariously trundles off down the track. Then, piling into the car with dogs and rods, we race for the coast in need of a cleansing dip in the sea. Smelling the salty wind through cracks in the hills, my brothers and I tumble down the cliff and dive into the freezing embrace. Washing off the dust and itchy grasses from our sun-beaten skin, we float on waves borne by the wind before collapsing back on the shore to stare at the unbroken sky in contented silence.

I spend a lot of time on the coast at this time of year, watching thunderous clouds prowl on the distant horizon as summer storms shimmer in the pink light and mackerel shoals swirl in the shadows underneath. Clambering on to the rocks with friends, we spend long evenings fishing for seabass and mackerel, cooking them over driftwood fires when we get lucky, but heading for vinegar-soaked fish and chips when we don't. Some days we leave with pockets and tackle boxes bursting with blue-striped mackerel and spend hours over the sink at home gutting the fish with music blaring as a few fillets spit on the stove for dinner.

The food of summer is immediate and vibrant, inspired by produce at its peak overflowing from the veg patch. The kitchen is filled with baskets of courgettes, among jugs of basil and mint, as we pod peas and broad beans at the table. Nectarines, peaches, gooseberries and apricots come back from the farm shop and it's rare that we aren't cooking outside in the garden under the warm twilight sky. Eating by candlelight, enjoying the quiet spell of the stars above and the bucolic bliss of an English summer.

AJO BLANCO
with summer vegetables, mint & lemon

AJO BLANCO IS A COLD ALMOND SOUP FROM SOUTHERN SPAIN that dates back to Moorish times and is thought to be a precursor to gazpacho. It's usually served ice cold with a drizzle of olive oil and some grapes or melon, but it also makes a wonderful sauce for veg, meat or fish. The key is to blitz the almonds for a long time on their own first so they release their oils and begin to get wonderfully smooth. Then you thin down with the water and olive oil to create a velvety texture. Sherry vinegar is a key ingredient here and you want to be quite generous with it at the end to get the balance right, but a quality red wine vinegar would also work if you don't have sherry vinegar. This recipe makes a generous amount of sauce, which will happily keep in the fridge for a week. If you want to make the more traditional soup, just let it down further with water and serve ice cold, with melon, olive oil and a few slivers of Ibérico ham.

SERVES 4

220g blanched almonds
  (ideally Spanish Marcona
  almonds)

200ml cold water

½ large cucumber, peeled
  and roughly chopped

2 cloves of garlic

150ml good olive oil

sherry vinegar, to taste
  (1–2 tbsp)

for the summer vegetables

4 tbsp olive oil

400g courgettes, thinly
  sliced

3 cloves of garlic, finely
  chopped

350g green beans

150g frozen peas
  (or 300g fresh peas)

1 lemon

a small bunch of fresh mint,
  leaves roughly torn

Start by toasting the almonds at 160°C fan for about 10 minutes, until they have the faintest gilding of gold. This accentuates their flavour and activates the oils, but don't take it too far or the flavour becomes quite overpowering. Leave to cool, then place in a food processor and blitz for about 10 minutes, scraping down the sides often and giving the machine a break if it's starting to overheat. Once the almonds are as smooth as you can get them, with the processor running, start trickling in the cold water until you have a thick double cream consistency (you may not need all the water). Then add the cucumber, grate in the garlic and blitz again. Finally, with the processor running, trickle in the olive oil. This will make the sauce wonderfully velvety and thick. Then season well with the vinegar and salt, this is a key moment. Blitz again and keep tasting and adjusting the seasoning as needed. You can let it down with more water if you feel it's too thick, and a bit of stale white bread will thicken it if it's gone too thin.

For the veg, get a pan of salted water on to boil for the beans. Heat the olive oil in a large pan and, once warm, add the courgettes, garlic and a generous pinch of salt. As the courgettes fry, cook the beans in the salted water for about 5 minutes, making sure they retain a lovely bite. Drain the

beans, then add to the softened courgettes along with the
peas. Toss this medley in the garlicky oil and cook until
the peas are bright green and tender. Now squeeze in some
lemon juice, add the mint and give it a good stir. Have a
taste – it should be zingy, crunchy, crisp and delicious.
Adjust with more salt and lemon as needed. Serve warm
on a puddle of the ajo blanco with a smattering of pepper.
I highly recommend turning any leftover sauce into the
traditional soup mentioned above. You don't need much, as
it's very rich, but it's perfect in a shot glass on a blisteringly
hot summer's day.

NECTARINE, MOZZARELLA & BASIL

THE BEAUTY OF THIS DISH LIES IN ITS SIMPLICITY and all boils down to the quality of one ingredient – the nectarines. The difference between a ripe nectarine and an unripe one is stark. Biting into a ripe nectarine is nothing short of sheer joy: it should burst with juice, balanced by a gentle acidity, and have the most glorious texture. It should not crunch. Buy a few more than you need for the recipe and try one – if they're not quite ready, just wait a few days.

When you've got an ingredient this good it's all about keeping it simple and I can't think of much better on a searingly hot day than this salad. Basil used like lettuce in vast quantities, the sweet nectarine singing with vinegar, the fatty luxuriousness of mozzarella and gentle spice of rocket and nasturtium. It's a harmony of flavour and utter bliss. Ideal as a light lunch in the heat with some good bread and prosciutto.

SERVES 4

4 perfectly ripe nectarines

4 balls of great mozzarella

a large bunch of fresh basil (think of it as a lettuce)

a small handful of spicy leaves – rocket, nasturtium flowers or Japanese mustards

1–2 tbsp really light and fruity vinegar (I like moscatel, or the Belazu fig leaf vinegar, which is niche but incredible, or any quality vinegar you have to hand)

½ lemon

a generous glug of olive oil, about 3 tbsp

Cut the nectarines in half around the stone, following the groove of the fruit. Twist each half and they should easily come away, as should the stone. If this is difficult, it's a sign they're not quite ripe. Cut the nectarine halves into jaunty chunks and place in a bowl, then roughly tear in the mozzarella. Add the basil leaves, spicy leaves, a little squeeze of lemon juice, a generous glug of olive oil and a splash of vinegar. Please, with flavours so delicate, don't go drowning this lovely salad in a throat-stripping vinegar. With simple food, the quality of your ingredients is ever more important. Go gently and find the perfect balance.

Season well with salt and pepper, then gently toss the salad a few times to distribute the dressing. Have a taste, get that perfect mouthful of basil, nectarine and mozzarella, and adjust the seasoning as necessary. Serve immediately – this does not want to hang around.

COURGETTE FRITTATA
with goat's cheese, lemon & mint

A FRITTATA MAKES FOR AN EFFORTLESSLY LIGHT LUNCH on a warm day with much to do. The key to a good frittata is taking it out of the oven at just the right time. You want the eggs to have only just cooked through and still be wonderfully juicy and fluffy. It's just as good cold for a picnic as it is warm, eaten on your knees in the garden with a zingy green salad. This version is brimming with slow-cooked garlicky courgettes, handfuls of fresh mint and dollops of goat's cheese, but it's one of those recipes that once you've got the hang of it you can play around with the filling depending on the season.

SERVES 4–6

5 tbsp olive oil

500g courgettes, sliced into rounds or halves no thicker than your little finger

3 cloves of garlic, finely sliced

150g frozen peas (or 300g fresh if you have them)

1 gem lettuce, halved and finely sliced

8 eggs

1 unwaxed lemon

10g fresh mint, leaves picked and roughly chopped

100g crumbly goat's cheese, mascarpone, ricotta or even crème fraîche

Preheat your oven to 200°C fan.

Place a large frying pan on a high heat, drizzle in about 4 tablespoons of olive oil and add the courgettes. Season well with salt and fry for about 5 minutes, until they begin to soften. The aim is to cook the courgettes quickly but not let them take on any colour or lose their texture. Add the garlic and give the pan a good toss, then let the garlic sizzle and infuse into the oil for a few minutes, by which point the courgettes should be perfectly tender. Add the peas and toss again to coat in the oil. Once they're sweet and cooked through, add the lettuce and stir. You only want to barely cook the lettuce, just letting it collapse into the medley.

Crack the eggs into a large bowl, grate in the lemon zest, chuck in the mint and whisk together. Taste the courgette mix to make sure the seasoning is spot on, then pour into the bowl, season again now you've added it to the eggs, and briefly mix together. Wipe away any bits that are stuck to the pan, then place on a medium-high heat and add a dash more olive oil to prevent sticking later on. Pour in the eggs, scraping out the bowl to get every last bit, then give the pan a shimmy to make sure it's sitting evenly. The aim here is to quickly cook and gently caramelise the bottom before it goes into the oven – think of gold, not brown. You will see the sides begin to bubble and crisp, and you can gently look underneath to check the colour with a spatula.

Crumble over the goat's cheese, or dot with mascarpone, ricotta or crème fraîche, and place in the oven

for just a few minutes, as it doesn't take long to cook the top. Intermittently check by giving the pan a jiggle, and when it's set, remove from the oven and run a spatula around the sides to gently unstick. Place a large chopping board on top of the pan and carefully but confidently invert while firmly holding the board; you should feel the frittata release. Either eat warm straight away, or leave to cool, slice and serve with a squeeze of lemon.

COURGETTE FLOWERS FILLED WITH A HERBY RICOTTA & BAKED IN TOMATO SAUCE

BY JULY THE ONSLAUGHT OF COURGETTES BEGINS. We plant them in great numbers, as they're tough as old boots and unbelievably productive, with each plant providing at least 30 courgettes through the season. The entire plant is edible, even the spiky leaves and the stalks, but the hidden gem is the flowers. Everyone loves them deep-fried, but here is something a bit different: we stuff the flowers, much like ravioli, and bake them in a rich tomato sauce. The result is a delicate mouthful of poached ricotta and herbs barely held together by the lightest of flowers. Mozzarella or goat's curd also make a fantastic filling.

SERVES 4

for the tomato sauce
3 tbsp olive oil
1 large brown onion, finely diced
3 cloves of garlic, smashed and peeled
2 x 400g tins of plum tomatoes
1 tsp caster sugar, if needed

for the courgette flowers
250g ricotta
a bunch of fresh basil, finely chopped, plus extra leaves for serving
a bunch of fresh mint or marjoram, leaves picked and finely chopped
1 large unwaxed lemon
20g parmesan, plus extra for serving
12 courgette flowers
1 tbsp olive oil

Start by making the tomato sauce. Heat the olive oil in a shallow ovenproof pan (one you can eventually bake the courgette flowers in) and, once warm, add the onion with a generous pinch of salt. Fry for 10–15 minutes, until sweet and tender, then add the garlic and fry for a few more minutes to infuse the oil. Pour in the tomatoes and break them up with a wooden spoon, then rinse out the tins with a splash of water and add this too. Season again and gently simmer for about 20 minutes, stirring occasionally, until rich and thickened.

While the tomato is simmering, crack on with stuffing the flowers. Put the ricotta into a bowl and whisk until smooth. Add the herbs, squeeze in a dash of lemon juice, grate in the parmesan and lemon zest and season well with salt and pepper. Mix well to combine, then taste and adjust the seasoning as necessary – it should be fantastic.

Preheat your oven to 200°C fan. If you look inside each courgette flower you will see the stamen – carefully, so you don't tear the flower, wiggle until it snaps and remove. Gently open up the flower and add a heaped teaspoon of the ricotta mix. Then either fold the petals over themselves or twist to seal in the ricotta. Repeat with the rest.

By now the tomato sauce should be ready. Taste for seasoning and add a teaspoon of caster sugar to balance out the acidity (if needed). Nestle the stuffed courgette flowers into the sauce, drizzle with a little olive oil, then put the lid on the pan and bake for 20 minutes.

Serve with a spoon or two of the tomato sauce. Finish with olive oil, fresh basil and a smattering of parmesan.

COURGETTE PASTA
with mascarpone, basil & lemon

HOMEGROWN COURGETTES COOKING IN A PUDDLE OF GOOD OLIVE OIL with garlic, lemon and chilli is a combination that sings of summer to me. I make this almost every day from June to September, to be stirred through risotto, served next to a piece of fish, on toast with burrata, or with my eggs in the morning. But my personal favourite is tossed through pasta with mascarpone, fresh basil and lemon. It's sheer joy, zingy and fresh with a gentle hum of chilli. Pictured here with homemade cavatelli, a much-loved pasta that's incredibly easy to make, with a pleasing texture that goes so well with this dish.

SERVES 4

1kg courgettes (ideally a few different colours, shapes and sizes)

5 tbsp olive oil

4 large cloves of garlic, finely sliced

a generous pinch of chilli flakes

400g pasta (I love using homemade cavatelli for this (see overleaf) but penne, tortiglioni and linguine are also great)

1 large unwaxed lemon

3 tbsp mascarpone

a large bunch of fresh basil, leaves picked (mint also works very well)

a knob of butter, about 30g

Start by bringing a large pan of well-seasoned water to the boil for the pasta.

Slice the courgettes into rounds about as thick as your little finger, cutting any large courgettes in half lengthways first. Heat the olive oil in a wide pan and add the courgettes. Season well with salt to draw out the moisture and fry for 5 minutes to get things going, before adding the garlic and chilli flakes. The key here is to end up with courgettes that are softened but not mushy, some beginning to collapse while others still have a bit of bite. The oil should be richly infused with garlic that has sweetened and not taken on any colour. Keep stirring the courgettes, and meanwhile get the pasta in.

When the pasta is al dente, remove a large mug of starchy water from the pan before straining. Add the pasta to the courgettes, grate in the lemon zest, then add the mascarpone and a generous splash of the reserved pasta water. Mix vigorously until the sauce is well combined and coats the pasta, adding more pasta water and mascarpone as needed. Squeeze in the juice of half the lemon, then add the basil and butter. Mix again and taste to check your seasoning – it may need a splash more lemon juice and salt. Serve immediately with a drizzle of really good olive oil.

HOMEMADE CAVATELLI

THIS TYPE OF HOMEMADE PASTA HAILS FROM THE SOUTH OF ITALY and is incredibly useful to know as it uses just two ingredients – flour and water – and requires no pasta machines to roll out. It's something I often make with friends, chatting away in the sun, with the dough in front of us, each rolling out our own portions of pasta. But it's not just fun to make; I love the texture of this eggless pasta, it has a lovely chew and bite that goes so well with many sauces. You can also use this dough to make pici, orecchiette and trofie as well as many other shapes. Watch some videos on how to roll those out, it's all in the movement of your hands.

SERVES 4

400g semolina flour

(I like to use a mix of half fine semolina, and half quality 00 flour for the best texture: Gilchesters semolina is particularly incredible for this)

200ml warm water

Pour the flour into a bowl. (You can use any flour – try experimenting with different wheats, different combinations etc. Even bog-standard plain flour will work if it's all you've got.) Get the water hot but not so hot you can't dip your finger into it. Pour this over the flour and season with a pinch of salt. Using a chopstick or the stick end of a wooden spoon, mix together until it forms a shaggy dough. Tip out on to your work surface and knead into a ball for just a few minutes. Cover with a damp tea towel and leave to rest for 20 minutes.

After 20 minutes you will feel that the once firm ball has now relaxed. Take a small pea-size piece and roll it against the grooves of a butter paddle or fork, to sort of curl it over on itself. You can even make these by just rolling the dough against your work surface. I would recommend watching a video online just to see the action. If there are a few of you working together this won't take long at all. Keep the dough covered with a tea towel to stop if drying out and make sure your work surface has some semolina on it to stop the cavatelli from sticking. You can roll out little snakes of dough, as pictured, and then chop into pea-size pieces ready to roll for speed and efficiency.

To cook, simply drop into seasoned boiling water and simmer for 3–5 minutes, until tender but with a nice bit of bite. Scoop out with a slotted spoon and combine with your sauce and a splash of the starchy pasta water.

ROMESCO
with burrata & grilled onions

ROMESCO IS ONE OF THE WORLD'S GREAT SAUCES. Hailing from Spain, it's made from toasted almonds, roasted red peppers, smoked paprika, chilli and vinegar. It's fatty, smoky, sweet and rich, with a lovely texture, and it goes with just about anything. Incredible with lamb, divine next to fish, roast chicken, eggs; there's not much I'd rather dunk a piece of bread into. Let's just say this is a sauce worth knowing how to make and a great thing to have in the fridge. Here I've suggested serving it with grilled onions and burrata, which with a piece of bread to dip and dunk makes a pretty punchy starter or light lunch.

SERVES 6

3 burrata

juice of ½ lemon

for the romesco

200g blanched almonds

6 red peppers (I tend to use Romano)

a jar of quality red roasted peppers, drained (300–400g)

80g sun-dried tomatoes

2 tsp sweet smoked paprika

1–2 tsp Aleppo chilli (or a pinch of chilli flakes for some gentle heat)

2 cloves of garlic

zest of 1 unwaxed lemon, juice of ½

2 tbsp moscatel or sherry vinegar

for the onions

6 medium onions

olive oil

splash of vinegar

Start by roasting the almonds in a 180°C fan oven for about 10 minutes. Keep an eye on them, as they can burn in a matter of seconds. Every now and then give the tray a jiggle to make sure they cook evenly.

Get the 6 Romano peppers into a roasting tray, drizzle with a glug of olive oil and season well with salt. You can grill them in the oven or on a griddle, or whack them on the barbecue, which adds a lovely smoky depth. Char them all over and when they begin to soften and collapse, place in a bowl and cover with a plate to form a seal. A tupperware box works well too. Leave them to steam for 20 minutes, then remove the skins and seeds.

I always use a food processor for this, but a pestle and mortar works too. Whack in all the romesco ingredients, but hold back on half the almonds and the vinegar. A good romesco has a lovely texture to it, with a nice crunch from the almonds. So the aim is to blitz/pound it as little as need be, while also making sure the flavours are well mixed. When it's well combined, add the rest of the almonds and briefly blitz or pound them to find the right consistency. Now taste. Add a pinch or two of salt and a splash of vinegar, stir this through and taste again. Keep adjusting until you have the seasoning right. Store in an airtight container; it freezes well, or will keep for a week or so in the fridge.

Cut the onions in half and pan-fry in olive oil, cut side down, until caramelised. Pour in a splash of vinegar, then

place the pan in a 200°C oven for about 30 minutes, until the
onions are tender.

   Put half a burrata on each plate, season with salt and
lemon juice and serve with a generous spoon of romesco
and the grilled onions ... bliss.

RATATOUILLE GALETTE
with anchovy & ricotta

I LOVE A GALETTE. THEY ARE BRILLIANTLY RUSTIC TARTS MADE WITH FLAKY PASTRY that are quick to throw together with no blind-baking faff. This one is first layered with whipped lemony ricotta and onions slow-cooked with anchovy, then finished in concentric circles of sliced courgettes, crisp meaty aubergines and slivers of tomato and garlic. It tastes even better than it looks and there's a joy in the methodical preparation. You do need to make the pastry on page 310, but luckily it couldn't be easier and is more than worth it.

SERVES 6–8

2 large aubergines, sliced into 1cm rounds

6 tbsp olive oil

2 large brown onions, finely diced

5–7 anchovies

250g ricotta

a small bunch of fresh thyme, leaves picked and finely chopped

1 unwaxed lemon

galette pastry (see page 310)

500g really good plum tomatoes, sliced into 1cm rounds

300g courgettes, sliced into 1cm rounds

2 cloves of garlic, finely sliced

a smattering of dried oregano

a scattering of fennel seeds

1 egg, beaten

Preheat your oven to 200°C fan. Line two baking trays with baking parchment. Place the aubergine slices on the lined trays and brush both sides with olive oil. Season with salt and bake in the oven for 20–25 minutes, until golden.

As the aubergine cooks, fry the onions with 3 tablespoons of olive oil and a pinch of salt for 15 minutes, until very soft and golden. Stir through the anchovies and allow them to melt into the onions. Remove from the heat and set aside to cool.

Put the ricotta, thyme and a pinch of salt into a mixing bowl. Grate in the lemon zest and squeeze in a little juice. Whisk until light and silky. Taste for seasoning and adjust.

Roll out the pastry with a little flour on a sheet of baking parchment into a wide disk about 4–5mm thick. When rolled out, carefully pull the parchment and pastry on to a sufficiently large tray. Then spread the ricotta over the pastry, leaving a 6–8cm border all the way round and spread the onions evenly over the ricotta.

Now working in concentric circles from the outside in, place a piece of tomato, followed by a courgette, then an aubergine. Go right the way round in a beautiful spiralling pattern, and every now and then sneak a sliver of garlic in between the tomatoes. When finished, drizzle with olive oil, season with salt and sprinkle over a little oregano and fennel seed. Fold over the edges of the pastry, then brush with the egg and place in the oven for 30–40 minutes, until the pastry is crisp and the veg is sizzling. Remove, leave to cool for a few minutes, then slice and serve.

MEDITERRANEAN FISH & CHIPS

THIS RECIPE TRANSPORTS ME STRAIGHT TO GREECE, a simple restaurant perched on a jagged cliff above the emerald sea. Octopus hang on a clothes line in the sun and the smell of charcoal and lamb fat carries on the salty wind. A pack of playing cards sits on the table with grilled fish straight from the sea, served simply with fried potatoes, lemon and jaw-dropping tomatoes. It's a dish I love so much that it would be sad to only eat it on my rare holidays. Here's how to make it at home.

Ideally, you'd cook the fish over charcoal outside in the sun, but roasting it in the oven works well too. Red mullet is a particular favourite, but I'd just ask your fishmonger what's fresh that day.

SERVES 4

4 red mullet

olive oil

aïoli (see page 307)

1 lemon, cut into wedges, for serving

for the oven chips

1kg potatoes (like Cyprus or Maris Piper), cut into 1.5–2cm thick chips

4 tbsp olive oil

a few sprigs of fresh rosemary, leaves stripped and finely chopped

for the tomato salad

500g of the best tomatoes you can find, in jaunty chunks

2 tbsp capers

½ red onion, very finely diced

1–2 tbsp quality red wine vinegar

2 tbsp best olive oil

Preheat your oven to 220°C fan. Line one or two large baking trays with baking parchment. Toss the potatoes with the olive oil and a generous pinch of salt, then spread out over the trays, making sure they are evenly spaced. Bake for 20–30 minutes, until golden and crisp at the edges, then turn and bake for a further 10–15 minutes on the other side. These are best when still chewy and soft with crisp edges; don't be tempted to take them too far.

As the chips bake, light the fire and prepare the tomato salad by simply mixing the ingredients in a bowl, seasoning and adjusting to taste.

Once the coals of the fire are hot but softened (you should be able to hover your hand over the heat for 3–5 seconds), rub the fish with a little olive oil and lay it on the grill. Cook for a few minutes on each side, depending on the thickness, and don't turn the fish until the skin is happy to release – if you have a fish basket, it will make this incredibly easy. Poke a skewer or sharp knife into the deepest point of the fish, leave for a few seconds, then put it to your lip. If it is warm, the fish is cooked.

When the chips are golden and crisp, remove them from the oven and immediately sprinkle over the finely chopped rosemary.

Serve the fish with the hot chips, tomato salad, aïoli and lemon wedges.

PAN CON TOMATE
with grilled sardines & salsa verde

I SPEND A LOT OF MY SUMMER AND AUTUMN FISHING. On a fine evening when the tide is right, it's rare that I don't nip to the coast with the dogs, my rod and a few cold beers. We fish off the rocks at the end of the beach, hoping for seabass but usually coming home with a few mackerel. Sometimes we cook them right on the beach, but more often than not they're in the pan the second we get home. This came from one of those evenings, so whether it's a fillet of fresh mackerel or sardines, just find the best tomatoes you can, and use some ciabatta or fresh sourdough to make this pan con tomate. How something so simple can be so extraordinarily delicious never ceases to amaze me.

To write an exact recipe for this seems a disservice to such an instinctive and simple dish . . . so this is more of a way than a method and it's the first thing I make when the good tomatoes are back in season. (*Pictured overleaf.*)

SERVES 4

4 of the best large tomatoes you can find

lots of extra virgin olive oil

12 fresh whole sardines or 4 spanking mackerel fillets

a loaf of sourdough or a couple of ciabattas

2 cloves of garlic

salsa verde (see page 307), for serving

If you're using sardines, I highly recommend cooking them over charcoal on the barbecue. But they are also fantastic cooked under the grill of your oven. If using mackerel fillets, I think they're best pan-fried briefly in a little olive oil.

On the large side of a box grater, grate the tomatoes into a bowl – you should find that you get left with the pulp in the bowl, and the skin in your hand. Discard the skin. Pour the tomato pulp into a sieve and just let it drip for 10–15 seconds; this gets rid of excess water, which will ruin the crispness of your toast faster than you can eat it. I collect this tomato water and usually drink it there and then. But it makes a great base for ceviche or the beginnings of quite an intriguing shot of Bloody Mary.

Now back to the tomato pulp – drizzle in a generous glug of olive oil and season well with salt. Have a taste, it should be amazing.

Brush your sardines or mackerel fillets with a splash of olive oil and season with a generous pinch of flaky salt. When the charcoal has died down on the barbecue and you can hold your hand over the heat for 3–5 seconds, place the sardines on the rack (ideally in a fish basket for easy turning) and cook for just a few minutes each side. The skin should blister and crackle and the dripping oils will create lovely whisps of smoke as they hit the coals. Mackerel are great cooked on the barbecue in a similar way, but generally I tend to fry the fillets in a pan with olive oil. Cook most of the way skin side down, for just a few minutes, at which point you will see the cookedness creeping up the sides of the fish. Briefly flip for about 10 seconds and serve immediately.

While the fish is cooking, timing is key. If using sourdough, slice and fry in a little olive oil until crisp on both sides (you can also just toast it). If using ciabatta, just cut in half horizontally and roast in the oven at 200°C fan until crisp. When the toast is ready, while still hot, rub generously with raw garlic, then spoon over a lavish amount of the tomato. Serve with the grilled fish and a spoon of salsa verde. Eat immediately!

SCALLOPS GRILLED IN THEIR SHELLS
with 'nduja butter

THIS IS ONE OF THOSE SPECIAL RECIPES THAT IS AS MUCH ABOUT THE ACT, the place and the adventure as it is the cooking itself. Here in Dorset the coast is covered with scallops and I have a great local friend who makes a living diving for them by hand in scuba gear off a little boat.

When they're as fresh as they are from Ali, often caught that day, the sweetness is extraordinary, so you don't want anything to distract from their delicate flavour. My favourite way is to make a simple flavoured butter, keeping the scallops in their shells to be used like little frying pans and cooking them directly in the embers of a fire by the sea. It's one of those moments where food is the starting point and core of something so much bigger and indescribable. The meeting point and relationship between nature and ourselves.

SERVES 4

250g unsalted butter, at room temperature

30g 'nduja

2 cloves of garlic

1 unwaxed lemon

12 scallops in their shells

for serving

a small bunch of fresh chives, finely chopped

a loaf of bread and something cold and delicious to drink

Start by making the 'nduja butter. Chuck the butter and 'nduja into a bowl or food processor. Grate in the garlic and the zest of the lemon. Squeeze in a little lemon juice, season with flaky salt and mix thoroughly to combine. Try a little on toast to check the seasoning and adjust with more lemon and salt as necessary. This can be made a few days in advance and stored in the fridge – I either roll it up with some baking parchment or keep it tightly in Tupperware. It can also be frozen, to last for many months.

Assuming you are doing this over fire and have the scallops ready with their shells, light a fire with a little dry wood and charcoal. Let it burn away until it glows, then when it begins to relax and the coals go white with ash, the heat has softened and it's ready to cook on.

Spoon a generous tablespoon of butter on to each scallop, then spread out the coals and place the shells carefully in the embers so that when the butter melts it doesn't just pour out. Grill the scallops for about 3 minutes, until the butter is bubbling enthusiastically, turning them halfway through. They really don't need long. Carefully take the shells from the fire with a pair of tongs and serve with a squeeze of lemon, a sprinkling of chives and a hunk of bread to scoop up the butter.

If you can't find the shells, you can of course use a frying pan and cook the scallops over a fire in just the same way as above. If fire isn't an option, the shells can be placed in a 200°C fan oven at home for 3–5 minutes, basting and turning the scallops halfway through until the butter melts and they're cooked to perfection. Without shells, simply pat the scallops dry and fry in a pan with olive oil for just a minute or so each side, then dollop in the butter and baste the scallops as it melts.

PAN-FRIED FISH
with courgette, white beans & basil

THIS DISH IS ALL ABOUT THE COURGETTE AND BEANS. I've served them with fish here, but it's a great side that we make all summer as it goes with just about anything. Courgettes gently cooked in lots of olive oil with garlic, lemon zest and chilli. Then stirred through creamy white beans and finished with a proper handful of basil, barely wilted and exploding with flavour. Heaven! Great piled on buttery sourdough, delicious with lamb cutlets, but particularly good with a delicate fillet of white flaky fish.

SERVES 4

for the courgettes and beans

500g courgettes (ideally 4–5 small ones in different colours)

4 tbsp olive oil

3 cloves of garlic, thinly sliced

a pinch of chilli flakes

1 unwaxed lemon

1 x 700g jar of quality white beans

a bunch of fresh basil, leaves picked

for the fish

4 fillets of firm white fish, such as turbot, halibut, seabass or pollack

2 tbsp olive oil

aïoli (see recipe on page 307), optional

Slice the courgettes into rounds no thicker than your little finger. If they are large, slice in half lengthways first. Pour the olive oil into a wide pan on a medium heat and, once shimmering, add the courgettes. Season well with salt and stir to coat in the oil. Once a bit of moisture has been released from the courgettes and the pan is bubbling, add the garlic and chilli flakes. With a potato peeler, peel the zest from the lemon, being careful not to go too deep, as the white is bitter. Then slice with a knife into very small slivers. This is essentially doing the work of a zester, but is a little chunkier so you really notice when you bite into a piece. Add this to the courgettes and cook for about 10–15 minutes, stirring occasionally, until the first courgettes begin to collapse. At this point, add the beans with all their liquid, stir through the courgettes and cook for a further 5 minutes so the flavours come together. Have a taste and adjust the seasoning as necessary. Set aside while you fry the fish.

For the fish, thoroughly dry the skin, drizzle with olive oil and season well with salt. Get a non-stick pan good and hot. Place the fish in the pan skin side down. It will sizzle fiercely – really press it into the pan to get a crispy skin. You want to cook the fish 75% on this side; how long this takes depends on the thickness of your fish, but you should be able to watch the cooked edges begin to creep up the side of the fish. When the skin stops sticking, you know it's crisp enough to be flipped. Turn and cook on the other side for just a minute or two tops. To test if the fish is cooked, take a knife or skewer and press it into the centre of the fish for a

few seconds, then bring it out and touch it to your lip. If it's warm, the fish is cooked; if it's hot, you've gone too far.

Make sure the beans are good and warm, then stir in the basil and serve with the fish, a squeeze of lemon and a dollop of aïoli, if you have it to hand.

SALMORIGLIO & SEABASS LINGUINE

SALMORIGLIO IS A SICILIAN SAUCE OF DRIED OREGANO, OLIVE OIL, GARLIC AND LEMON. It's a strong summery sauce, quick to make and singing with flavour. Particularly good spooned over steamed or grilled vegetables, barbecued fish and lamb cutlets, it also works well as a marinade and is a great thing to have in your toolkit. Here I've used it as a delicate pasta sauce with flaked seabass and parsley. Imagine a Sicilian-inspired aglio e olio (spaghetti with garlic, chilli and olive oil), but with tender flakes of fish and a ton of parsley, this is a wonderfully light and zingy summer pasta that's quick to throw together. The texture of seabass works particularly well here, but you can use any flaky white fish.

SERVES 3

300g linguine

300g fresh seabass fillets

2 tbsp olive oil

a decent-sized bunch of parsley, finely chopped

for the salmoriglio

2 cloves of garlic

120ml olive oil

the juice of 1 lemon, about 60ml

a generous pinch of quality dried oregano

a pinch of chilli flakes

Start by getting a pan of water on to boil for the pasta, then make the salmoriglio. Put all the ingredients for the sauce into a high-speed food processor and whiz until smooth. I like to do this in a Nutribullet, where it gets lovely and velvety, but you can use an immersion blender or simply grate the garlic into a jar followed by the rest of the ingredients and shake madly. Leave this to one side and the lemon will relax the rawness of the garlic.

Season the pasta water and get the linguine going. While the pasta is cooking, remove the skin from the fish and cut the fillets into small pieces. Place the fish in a bowl and season well with salt and pepper. Just a few minutes before the pasta is ready, get a wide shallow pan good and hot, drizzle in the olive oil and add the fish. Toss it in the oil and let it sizzle. When both sides have begun to turn white, add the pasta to the fish with a little splash of pasta water and the parsley. Pour over a generous amount of the salmoriglio, remembering you can always add more but never take it away, and mix well with the pasta water to form a silky sauce. Have a taste and adjust the seasoning as necessary. Eat immediately, with extra sauce at the table for anyone who wants a splash more.

LINGUINE VONGOLE

SPAGHETTI VONGOLE IS A LEGENDARY DISH, GENIUS IN ITS PURITY, the most traditional versions adamant in their simplicity to let the clams shine. I have such fond memories of Dad making it for us as kids with squid ink pasta, cherry tomatoes and fennel seeds for their added burst of sweetness.

This, on the other hand, is a more purist recipe, with no additions to distract from the wonderful marriage of clams, wine and garlic. The absolute key to vongole is the timing. You want the pasta perfectly al dente by the time it joins the clams, which have ideally only just opened and released their juices. The clever trick is a little knob of butter at the end, which adds a silky fattiness and helps emulsify the sauce. Some people don't serve it with lemon so as not to distract from the clams, but for me it's a must – a light grating of zest and squeeze of juice at the end really brings it to life.

SERVES 4

1kg fresh clams

400g linguine

4 tbsp olive oil

6 cloves of garlic, sliced paper thin

1 large red chilli, finely chopped, or a pinch or two of chilli flakes

100ml white wine

30g unsalted butter

a really large (20g) bunch of fresh parsley, finely chopped

1 large unwaxed lemon

Refresh the clams in a sink of water with a handful of salt and discard any that don't close.

Bring a large pot of generously salted water to the boil and chuck in the pasta – it's a fast dish, you've gotta keep up. Put the olive oil, garlic and chilli into another large pan, THEN turn the heat on; this way the oil slowly warms up and you get maximum infusion from the chilli and garlic. Let these gently sizzle in the oil for a few minutes, but don't let the garlic or chilli colour in the slightest. When the oil is smelling amazing, pour in the white wine and put the lid on the pan. Crank the heat to max and when the wine is steaming chuck in the clams. Put the lid back on and give the pan a good shake, then leave undisturbed for 2–3 minutes.

By now the pasta should be al dente and the clams beginning to open. Take a large mug of pasta water from the pot, then drain the pasta and immediately add it to the clams. Add a proper splash of pasta water, the butter and the parsley. Mix vigorously, tossing the pasta again and again to emulsify and coat the pasta in the sauce, of which you want lots. Squeeze in the juice of half a lemon and grate in a touch of lemon zest. Mix again, taste and adjust the seasoning as necessary. Serve immediately, with a drizzle of really good olive oil.

SPINACH, TOMATO & ANCHOVY GRATIN

A GOOD GRATIN IS A WONDERFUL THING — A HUMBLE DISH OF VEG baked in a creamy sauce with a crisp and caramelised top. Dauphinoise is of course the king of gratins, but it's a method I love to use for much more than just potatoes. Swiss chard, leeks, celeriac and turnips are all fantastic in a gratin. This is a summery version that is beloved at home. Great on its own with a sharp green salad, but punchy enough to be the perfect side to some lamb or a lovely cut of steak. I've used milk instead of cream, which gives the dish a lightness, but in the colder days of early autumn while the tomatoes are still good, I go half and half with some double cream for a hearty bit of added oomph.

SERVES 5–6

800g plum tomatoes, quartered lengthways

5 tbsp olive oil

800g spinach

50g butter

2 large brown onions, finely chopped

40g plain flour

a splash of white wine, about 100ml

500ml whole milk

⅔ nutmeg

10 anchovies

70g coarse fresh breadcrumbs

Preheat your oven to 200°C fan.

Nestle the tomatoes in your chosen dish or tray, into which they fit snugly in one layer – don't stack them on top of one another. Drizzle generously with about 2 tablespoons of olive oil and season well with salt. Roast in the oven for about 1 hour; the aim here is to concentrate the flavour and texture by cooking out some of the water.

While the tomatoes are cooking, wash the spinach thoroughly. Heat 2 tablespoons of olive oil in a large pan on a medium heat. Add the spinach, still a little wet from its wash, season with salt and cook for a few minutes, until wilted. You may need to do this in batches. Once wilted, transfer to a colander and leave to drain.

Return the pan to the heat and add the butter. Once melted, add the onions with a hefty pinch of salt and fry for about 15 minutes, until very soft. Add the flour and stir, then turn the heat down and cook out the flour for a few minutes, stirring regularly. Add a splash of white wine and whisk it through the flour – it will form a claggy paste. Slowly add the milk, a splash at a time, while whisking constantly. Doing this slowly and whisking thoroughly before adding the next glug assures you get no floury lumps. Once you've added all the milk, grate in the nutmeg, then season well with salt and pepper. Have a taste and adjust the seasoning.

CONTINUED OVERLEAF

It's important to get the béchamel correctly seasoned at this point or the dish will be bland later on.

By now the tomatoes should be ready, so remove them from the oven. Give the spinach a good squeeze to remove all the liquid, then add it to the tomatoes, nestling it around and among them. Pour over the béchamel and run a spoon around the tray, allowing the béchamel to seep its way in and around. Lay the anchovies evenly on top, scatter with the breadcrumbs and drizzle with a little olive oil. Place back in the oven for about 30 minutes, until the top is golden and the béchamel is bubbling. You can give it a short blast under the grill to get a little more colour if need be. Leave to sit for 10–15 minutes before tucking in.

GRILLED LAMB
with tapenade butter

THE FATTINESS OF LAMB SINGS WHEN PAIRED WITH STRONG, SALTY FLAVOURS. This tapenade butter is punchy, but really enhances the flavour of the lamb. You'll find yourself mopping up the juices, enjoying the aromatics of the rosemary and the richness of dark olives and anchovies. It's a dish I fell in love with one summer, but can be eaten year-round right into the darkest depths of winter – just play with the veg that you pair it with. One of my favourite ways, though, is to serve it with boiled fennel and new potatoes (see below), simply finished with olive oil and parsley.

This recipe makes quite a lot of the butter – roll it up in cling film or foil, and have it ready in the freezer for when you're in need of a burst of flavour. Fantastic alongside a steak, on toast with soft-boiled eggs, even spooned over a meaty piece of fish. If you don't want leftovers, just halve the butter recipe. (*Pictured overleaf.*)

SERVES 6

12 lamb chops

olive oil

a handful of fresh parsley, finely chopped

for the tapenade butter

1 jar of pitted Kalamata olives, about 160g when drained

100g capers

3 sprigs of fresh rosemary

250g salted butter, softened

10 anchovies

2–3 cloves of garlic, depending on their size

1 unwaxed lemon (zest for the butter and a little juice for serving)

Making the tapenade butter couldn't be simpler. Drain the olives and capers and let them dry in a sieve while you finely chop the rosemary. Put all the ingredients into a food processor, grating in the garlic and lemon zest, then pulse to combine. I like to keep quite a lot of texture in the olives and capers, so briefly blitz just to bring it together, scraping down the sides of the bowl a few times to make sure it's evenly incorporated. Save a few heaped tablespoons for the lamb chops, then roll the rest up in a log with some cling film and wrap in foil. This can then be sliced and used from frozen.

Season the lamb chops with salt, then leave them in a bowl for 30 minutes so the salt can penetrate the meat and they come to room temperature. When ready, get a frying pan on a medium heat, drizzle in a tiny splash of olive oil, then put in the chops standing fat side down. Balance them together and leave to sizzle for about 5 minutes, pressing down occasionally, until you have lovely caramelisation on the fat. Take them out for a second, turn the heat up to full blast and, once the pan is clearly very hot, put them back in and quickly sear each side until golden brown. When the second side is golden, chuck in 2 generous spoons of

CONTINUED OVERLEAF

the tapenade butter, shaking and shimmying the pan while spooning the butter over the chops. Then pour it all into a bowl, covering the lamb with all the butter, and leave to rest for 5 minutes. After the rest, season with a little squeeze of lemon, a smattering of pepper and a handful of finely chopped parsley. Hopefully you will have beautiful chops that are still pink and blushing in the middle, with crispy fat that just explodes with the salty rich flavours of the butter.

I particularly love this with fennel and boiled potatoes, one of my favourite sides. So here's just a rough sketch of how to throw that together – it's very easy and is also delicious with fish. While the lamb is coming up to room temperature with the salt, get a pan of well-seasoned water on to boil and drop in some really sweet new potatoes. After about 10 minutes, start the lamb cooking process, and roughly chop a similar amount of fennel to the new potatoes. When the spuds are nigh on ready, drop in the fennel – ideally at this point you would be taking the lamb off the heat to begin resting. Boil the fennel until tender, about 5 minutes, then strain off the water and season with a generous pinch of flaky salt, loads of olive oil, a squeeze of lemon and a handful of fresh parsley. Mix well, breaking up the potatoes a little with a spoon. Serve alongside the chops with lots of their butter. Sublime!

EASY CHICKEN TRAYBAKE

THIS IS MY GO-TO CHICKEN MARINADE, A FRAGRANT MIX OF HERBS AND SPICES with yoghurt, garlic and lemon. When left to sit for a while, a marinade helps to ensure juicy chicken, so if you can, give it time to work its magic. Most importantly, make sure you let the chicken come up to room temperature, don't cook it straight from the fridge. Start the oven off hot, but once you've got that lovely golden crust, turn the heat right down to slowly finish the cooking. Before serving, give the chicken a rest to reabsorb those juices.

SERVES 6

2 tbsp Aleppo chilli
  (a light, fragrant chilli)

2 tbsp fennel seeds

1 tbsp cumin seeds

2 tbsp dried oregano

20g flaky sea salt

6 cloves of garlic

6 tbsp yoghurt

2kg chicken thighs, wings
  and drumsticks

a bunch of fresh thyme

olive oil

1 unwaxed lemon

tahini sauce, spiced with a
  little cumin (see page 255)

I like to make the marinade in a pestle and mortar, where you can quickly bash it together, but a food processor or even just whacking it all in a bowl works well too. Put the spices, oregano and salt into your mortar and briefly grind together to break them down a bit. Add the garlic, grind to a fine paste, then add the yoghurt and mix together. Put the chicken into a large bowl and pour in the spiced yoghurt. Pick the leaves off the thyme and add to the bowl, then drizzle in some olive oil and massage the marinade into the chicken, making sure to work it into every nook and cranny. Ideally, you should leave this to sit covered for at least a few hours before cooking.

When ready to cook, remove the chicken from the fridge and leave to come up to room temperature. Preheat your oven to 230°C, on the fan-grill setting. Place some baking parchment on a large baking tray and cover with the chicken, scooping out any leftover marinade from the bowl and spreading it over the skin. Bake for around 15–20 minutes – you're looking for the skin to quickly caramelise but not burn. When the chicken has a nice colour, remove from the oven, baste with any juices and peel in the lemon zest. Turn the oven right down to 140°C fan and put the chicken back in for 10–15 minutes, until cooked. Remove and leave to rest for 10 minutes before tucking in. I particularly love this with a tahini sauce spiced with a little cumin.

STEAMED APRICOT SPONGE

A STEAMED SPONGE IS A GLORIOUS THING: effortless to make, juicy and light as air. These mini sponges are cooked with tart stewed apricots at the bottom of the moulds, which ooze into the sponge when flipped. Apricots are my favourite fruit for cooking, their tartness just heaven against the sweetness of the sponge. But the apricot season is short and this is a dish worth making throughout the year, so substitute in any stewed fruit – just make sure it's jammy and not too wet. In winter, marmalade makes a great replacement.

SERVES 4

for the stewed apricots

40g butter

6 apricots, halved and destoned

3 tbsp caster sugar

a splash of apple brandy, Madeira or any sweet booze

for the sponge

90g unsalted butter, at room temperature, plus extra for greasing

90g caster sugar

zest and juice of 1 unwaxed lemon

2 eggs, lightly beaten

115g self-raising flour

½ tsp baking powder

2 tbsp whole milk

for serving

homemade custard, ice cream, crème fraîche or double cream

Preheat your oven to 180°C fan and generously grease four 3 x 2 inch dariole moulds with butter. Start with the apricots. Put the butter into a pan that will fit the apricots snugly in one layer, then turn on the heat and when the butter begins to foam, add the apricots cut side down. Sprinkle over the sugar and cook for 4 minutes, until they begin to soften, then flip the apricots and pour in the brandy. Cook for a further 3 minutes, then turn the heat off and let them sit. You want them cooked enough that they're softened and have created a lovely syrup but aren't falling apart.

For the sponge, use a stand mixer or electric whisk to cream the butter, sugar and lemon zest for about 5 minutes, until pale and fluffy. With the mixer/whisk still running, slowly pour in the beaten eggs. Then sift in the flour and baking powder, fold together and stir through the milk and lemon juice.

Place three apricot halves and a generous spoonful of their syrup in the bottom of each mould. Top with the sponge mix but don't fill it right to the top, as they rise quite a long way up. Cover each mould with a circle of baking parchment. These can sit in the fridge until you want to cook them. Place the moulds in a high-sided baking tray and fill the tray with boiling water to come halfway up the moulds. Cover the tray tightly with foil and bake for 35–40 minutes. To test for doneness, insert a skewer into the centre of the sponge; it should come out clean. Remove from the oven, take off the baking parchment and run your knife around each sponge. Flip them into bowls and serve with homemade custard, ice cream, crème fraîche or double cream.

APRICOT TARTE TATIN

I HAVE BEEN MAKING THIS RECIPE FOR YEARS. Apricots are a great fruit to cook with as they come alive in the heat. This is an immediate and easy way to make the most of their sharp and jammy qualities. Where a traditional tart takes quite a lot of preparation, with blind baking and rolling out pastry, a tarte tatin has none of that faff as you cook the tart upside down. Once the filling has come together, which only takes moments with apricots, you simply whack the pastry on top, tuck in the edges and blast in the oven until crisp and puffed. Then enjoy the moment where you flip it out and reveal the glowing filling within.

SERVES 6

500–650g fresh apricots

40g butter

80g golden caster sugar

1 sheet of all-butter puff pastry or homemade rough puff pastry (see page 310)

1 egg, beaten

for serving

softly whipped cream, crème fraîche or ice cream

honey and fresh thyme leaves (optional)

Preheat your oven to 200°C fan.

First destone the apricots: run your knife along the groove, then twist the two sides and pop out the stone. Place a 25–30cm ovenproof frying pan on a medium heat and melt the butter. Place the apricots in, cut side down; you need enough to completely fill the pan, remembering they shrink as they cook, but not stacking them on top of each other. Sprinkle in the sugar and cook gently for a few minutes, shimmying the pan a bit so the sugar melts and the apricots release their juice, creating a sticky sauce. Turn over after not too long, as we want them to retain their texture in the oven.

Cut your pastry to a disk a touch wider than the pan. Off the heat, place the pastry on top of the apricots and tuck in the edges so the sides envelop the fruit. Brush with the egg, prick with a fork in a few places and place in the oven for 20–30 minutes, until the pastry is wonderfully golden and crisped. Remove from the oven and allow to cool for 5 minutes, then place a large plate or chopping board on top of the pan and carefully flip to turn out the tart. Serve with whipped cream, crème fraîche or ice cream. A little honey is sometimes nice drizzled on top too, with a smattering of fresh thyme.

SOUR CHERRY MADEIRA ICE CREAM

WHERE I USED TO LIVE, WE HAD THESE TWO TINY MORELLO CHERRY TREES. They were spindly little things that never grew taller than me, but they did produce a small bounty of delicious fruit each year, too sour to eat fresh but incredible for cooking and the reason this recipe was born. I have since adapted the recipe to use normal cherries, with a little added lemon juice to create that same tartness. But if you stumble across some morello cherries or are lucky enough to have a tree, make this recipe without the lemon and prepare to be amazed! Here the cherries are tart and chewy, mixing with a slightly burnt caramel to create a blood red syrup that is perfectly offset by the cooling vanilla-studded ice cream. Great in a cone, or just in a bowl, this recipe also works really well with damsons in autumn, just drop the lemon. If you don't have an ice cream machine or simply don't want to make ice cream, you could buy some good vanilla ice cream and spoon the sour Madeira cherries on top.

SERVES 6

for the cherry ripple
500g cherries
120g caster sugar
80ml Madeira
2 large lemons

for the vanilla ice cream
450ml double cream
375ml whole milk
1 vanilla pod
120g caster sugar
5 egg yolks

Start by making the custard for the ice cream. Pour the cream and milk into a heavy-based pan, then slice the vanilla pod in half lengthways, scrape out the seeds and add to the pan with the spent pod. Turn the pan on to a low heat and bring up to a gentle simmer. While the cream is heating, whisk the sugar with the egg yolks in a bowl until pale and fluffy. Now, little by little, pour the hot cream over the egg yolks, whisking constantly. This tempers the yolks, warming them up slowly so that the heat of cooking doesn't shock and scramble them.

Pour this mixture back into the pan and cook on a low heat, stirring constantly so that it doesn't sit on the bottom too long. Keep cooking and stirring until the mixture thickens enough that when you bring out your wooden spoon, you can draw a line through the custard on the back of the spoon and it doesn't run. To check with a temperature probe, it's ready when between 77°C and 82°C. Be careful not to overheat or it will curdle. Pour through a sieve to strain out any lumps, then place in the fridge to cool for at least 4 hours or overnight.

CONTINUED OVERLEAF

Now time for the cherries. You need to pit them, either with a cherry stoner or by running your knife around each cherry and twisting off the fruit. For the caramel, lightly sprinkle the sugar into a wide silver-coloured pan and place on a medium heat. Don't touch it. As the sugar begins to melt, turn and tilt the pan a little so that it melts evenly but do not stir. You want to keep cooking it until it begins to smoke and turn a nice red colour. This darker caramel has much more flavour. Now carefully pour in the Madeira: the cold will solidify the caramel, but as the Madeira heats up, the caramel will begin to melt into it. Add the cherries and cook until they collapse and leach their juices into the sauce. This takes about 15–20 minutes; by then they should be chewy and delicious. Squeeze in the juice of a lemon, stir through and taste – it may need balancing with a touch more lemon or sugar. The sourness is the perfect counterpart to the sweet ice cream.

Pour the cooled custard into your ice cream machine and follow the instructions. When ready, place in a Tupperware container and pour over the cherry mix. Ripple this through, then cover and leave to set in the freezer.

CUCUMBER & MINT
OR RASPBERRY LEMONADE

IT'S A SCORCHING DAY, WE'RE IN THE MIDST OF A HEATWAVE and it hasn't rained for weeks. There's not a cloud in the sky and a rippling heat is shimmering across the fields. Buzzards screech high above, their silhouettes like burnt shadows curving around the sun. The goats bask in the warmth while the sheep pant in the shade of the hedgerow. My two shaggy lurchers are plastered to the cold kitchen floor and I have an afternoon of stacking hay bales ahead. It's been a record year, 340 bales compared to the 240 last year. We spend the afternoon piling them high on the trailer, loading eight bales at a time from the tractor bucket. By the end the stack is as tall as the house and, while brutal, this is one of my favourite jobs of the year; coming together with our neighbours, making the most of luscious summer grasses to feed our animals through the leaner winter months. Once finished, we are sticky with sweat and covered in itchy grasses; leaving them collapsed in the shade of the trailer, I head inside to make the most refreshing drink I know – ice-cold lemonade. Here are my two favourites, cucumber and mint, and a Sicilian-inspired version using whole lemons and raspberry. (*Pictured overleaf.*)

CUCUMBER & MINT

MAKES ABOUT 1.5 LITRES
(8 GENEROUS GLASSES)

1 large cucumber, 500g, roughly chopped

flaky sea salt

4 lemons

100g caster sugar

10g fresh mint leaves (or even better, a few fresh lemon verbena leaves if you have some)

lots of ice, extra cucumber slices and fresh mint sprigs, for serving

Put the cucumber into a food processor with a pinch of sea salt and blitz for a minute into a paste. Pour this into a fine sieve set over a bowl to catch the juice and leave to drip for 15 minutes – you want as much of the cucumber liquid as possible. You can also just grate the cucumber into a sieve if you're keen not to use any equipment.

After 15 minutes, squeeze out any remaining juice from the cucumber and discard the pulp (I sometimes use it in a quick tzatziki). Juice the lemons through a sieve into the cucumber, getting as much juice as possible from each lemon. Then add the sugar to the mix and vigorously whisk until it dissolves. Have a taste – it should be pretty epic. I like to add a pinch of flaky sea salt at this point, which adds some much needed salinity, great for replacing electrolytes on a hot day. Chop the mint as fine as you can get it, then add it to the lemonade mix.

CONTINUED OVERLEAF

Fill a large jug to the brim with ice and pour in the lemonade mix to just under halfway. Top up with water and leave in the fridge to get properly cold. To serve, pour over more ice, with a few slices of cucumber, a sprig of mint and a touch more flaky sea salt.

PS This is also a fantastic base for a gin cocktail.

RASPBERRY

MAKES ABOUT 1.5 LITRES
(8 GENEROUS GLASSES)

4 unwaxed lemons

250g raspberries

150g caster sugar

10g fresh mint leaves

*lots of ice and extra fresh
mint sprigs, for serving*

Chop one of the lemons into quarters, carefully scoop out any pips, then put the whole lemon pieces into a blender with the raspberries and the sugar and blitz until completely smooth. Squeeze the juice of the remaining lemons through a sieve into the blender, add the mint and blitz again briefly to combine. You should now have a wonderfully voluptuous and vibrant pink mix that is at once sharp, sweet and tangy. Using a whole lemon is a Sicilian touch, which adds a gentle bitterness that wonderfully offsets the other flavours.

Fill a large jug to the brim with ice and pour in the pink lemonade mix to come just under halfway up. Top up with water and leave in the fridge to get properly cold. Stir vigorously before you serve, as this is a much thicker lemonade with all the pulp. Finish with a sprig or two of mint.

AUTUMN

Autumn, much like spring, is a season of stark transition, taking us from the vibrant bounty of summer back into the barren cold of winter. If you were to jump from the beginning to the end, the change would be vast, but it's a season that begins almost imperceptibly and much of autumn is a time of harvest and plenty, as we make the most of tomatoes, courgettes and fresh herbs before the leaner days of winter return. Hedges swell with dark fruit and purple fingers gather blackberries by the basket for pies and crumbles. The warm autumn rains have the dry summer grasses growing again and my sheep fatten in the fields as their fleeces begin to thicken ahead of winter. Our neighbour brings his cows down through our higher meadows to pull at the long pasture and spread the wildflower seeds. Sitting among them, I love their peaceful presence; chewing loudly, they swish at bothersome flies and watch me curiously with doleful eyes and sweet grassy breath. In the golden light of dawn, low mists hang in the valley and the dewy light illuminates a carpet of spider webs floating ethereally in the air. The end of September has the swallows gathering in their hundreds, swirling above the tufty meadows as they teach their young to fly while gorging on insects before their migration to Africa for winter.

In the garden, things are flourishing and all the hard work of spring is really paying off by now. Our tall hazel frames are thick with a jungle of dark green leaves that hide clusters of long crunchy beans underneath. Sunflowers stand tall, alive with bees that vibrate with joy in the yellow pollen. Jerusalem artichokes teeter in the wind as pumpkin vines escape their borders and climb the garden fence. It's now almost impossible to keep up with the supply of tomatoes in the polytunnel, and those left on the vine too long explode with juice. The courgettes are out of control and we fill wheelbarrows with endless marrows for the goats. In the greenhouse the shorter days have us planning ahead, sowing the last of the cabbages, leeks and kales to keep us fed through the dark frosts of winter.

Each day the sun hangs a little lower in the sky, and the honeyed light casts long shadows across the fields as a cool breeze sends us reaching for our first woolly jumpers of the season. In the orchard the trees are hanging heavy with the weight of fruit, and climbing high in the lichen-covered

branches I battle with hornets and wasps over dark plums and glowing quince. Great pots of jam simmer on the stove, the glossy bubbles bursting at the surface as we sterilise jars and pour in bags of sugar to preserve the abundance of fruit. The chillies we planted are finally fizzing with colour and we string them up to dry in the greenhouse with bundles of excess herbs and flowers. The first rosy apples appear on the gnarled trees and we cook them with overripe tomatoes to make spiced ketchups and sauces. Sharp damsons and bullace get covered with gin to infuse ahead of Christmas, and elderberries simmer away in a dark elixir called Pontack sauce. We do much pickling, fermenting, drying and infusing; the kitchen is alive with vinegary steam as we preserve those gluts in the garden that we can't keep up with, providing a welcome burst of colour in the leaner days of winter to come.

Autumn is the time for fishing. My brothers and I often head to the coast in the evenings and watch clouds of mackerel leaping from the water as they chase shoals of whitebait on to the shore. Before setting up our rods we'll run along and pick great handfuls of the little fish, to fry in spiced flour for a quick snack once home. Farmers come down with their sheepdogs, who zip up and down the shore eating them straight off the sand. On a good evening, with weighted feathers, we sling our hooks into the seething water and catch five mackerel at a time, going home with thirty shimmering fish for the smoker.

Then of course, the trees begin to fade and the woods become a canopy of rusty leaves that swirl and flutter in the breeze. I walk in a trance, scanning the forest floor for mushrooms, hunting for porcini and chanterelles while the dogs zip back and forth chasing squirrels around me. I still haven't quite found my reliable spot yet, but a neighbour drops round a bag of huge penny buns that we cook in foaming butter with garlic and fresh eggs for breakfast, always one of my most memorable meals of the year.

By October the nights are beginning to grow cold, but the days are still bright, green and sunny. It's a magical time of year, almost like a second spring. The nanny goats are beginning to get a little frisky and spend their days calling across the fields to my billies, who stand with heads high in the air, puffing and snorting as they catch their scent on the wind. Waking up one morning I find Leo, one of my mightiest billies, strutting around the yard on his way to find the girls and we spend ages trying to catch him with a bucket of food and lassos. This starts a trend, and every day there's an escapee as persistent billies ignore electric fences and jump six-foot gates; it's a nightmare. The worry is that they will get the nannies pregnant too early in the year, or even worse the kids, who are much too young. So we attach ropes to the naughtiest of the billies, which trail along the ground and make them easy to catch when they escape, and hide the girls up the hill where they can't be smelt or seen. But inevitably, each year there's always an early birth or two that takes us by surprise.

Towards the end of autumn, fierce storms begin to batter the farm, tearing the burnished leaves from the trees and flooding the veg patch. We light our first fires of the year and the house smells of warm smoke once again. The tomatoes and courgettes are still going but the food has changed from light and colourful, to slow and comforting against the cold. October shivers into November with iron skies and sharp winds. The grass begins to slow and my breath fogs, marking time to start putting hay out for the animals once again. We put the billies and rams in with the girls, who flee from their first excited attempts, as the boys strut among them with heads held high, spitting and snorting with great gusto. Eventually the first frost arrives, a sad day that brings an end to much of the veg as tender herbs, towering beans and courgettes wither into the ground with cold.

Apples fall to the ground in droves and so begins the first cider pressing of the year. With our neighbours we gather them in old compost bags and crush them in old tractor-powered machines to be layered with straw and slowly pressed by great oak beams in yeasty barns. The cloudy juice trickles into buckets as we laugh and sway with mugs of last year's cider in hand, collecting the sweet nectar in musky barrels to slowly ferment over winter.

Finally the dark closes in, and nature is laid bare once more. The daily routine of hay and feed commences again and nourishing pots of broth bubble on the stove. We are back to winter, a time of slowing down and taking stock, waiting until the cycle repeats again and thrusts us back into the chaos of spring. This is the joy of the seasons, embracing the change, relishing in the knowledge that what was good comes round once again. After all, 'What good is the warmth of summer, without the cold of winter to give it sweetness.[1]'

BEETROOT SOUP *&* THREE TOPPINGS

THIS IS ONE OF THOSE RECIPES MY FAMILY JUST LIVE OFF, a dish we return to again and again, at its heart deeply simple and uplifting. Velvety and voluptuous, this soup bubbles away like a cauldron of lava and is wonderfully nourishing. Seasoned with a little cider vinegar to brighten the earthy richness, it's a dinner party classic I often serve as a starter because of its striking colour, but it's equally at home eaten on your knees. I've given you three toppings that will bring this soup to life, so you can vary how you eat it depending on what you have to hand.

MAKES 8 PROPER
BOWLFULS

1.5kg beetroots

100ml cider vinegar

200ml crème fraîche or double cream

your choice of topping

a few slices of smoked eel and a dollop of fiery horseradish sauce (see page 308)

crumbly goat's cheese and dill

natural yoghurt and toasted cumin seeds

Start by giving the beets a good scrub in the sink to remove any grit. Don't peel or trim the tops; you want them intact, to preserve the vivid colour. Place in a large pan and cover with water, then pour in the vinegar and season with a proper handful of salt. Bring to the boil, then set to a simmer with the lid on for about 1 hour, until completely tender. You should be able to easily pierce them to the core with a knife.

Take the beets out and leave them to cool in a bowl, but keep all the cooking liquor. When cool enough to handle, peel off the skins: they should come away easily with a squeeze from your thumb – I think it's one of the most satisfying jobs in the kitchen, but wear a pair of Marigolds or your hands will be pink for days. Chop the beetroots into quarters and place in a high-speed blender, then top up with a little of the cooking water and blitz into a thick pourable soup. You might need to do this in two or three batches. Taste as you go, as you don't want to overdo it with the vinegary water, though the vinegar is a key part of the seasoning and cuts through excessive earthiness. Add the crème fraîche while blitzing in the blender and it will lighten and aerate the soup into a lovely velvety texture. It should taste divine and be the most incredible colour, but make sure to taste and adjust the seasoning to get the balance right.

Warm back up in a pan, and finish with your chosen toppings. This keeps in the fridge for up to a week, and you can freeze any leftovers for a rainy day.

PADRÓN, IBÉRICO HAM & EGGS ON TOAST

THIS DISH IS A RIOT OF FLAVOUR AND ABSOLUTELY DELICIOUS. More of an assembly than a recipe, it couldn't be easier to make. Blistered lemony Padrón peppers with slivers of nutty Iberico ham, chilli and a fried egg on buttery toast. Ideal for breakfast if you're feeling a little frail from the night before, but I'd happily eat this morning, noon and night. I particularly love finishing this with a few anchovies on top, but if you're not keen, just leave them out.

SERVES 3

3 tbsp olive oil

300g Padrón peppers

1 lemon

3 eggs

3 slices of sourdough or ciabatta

a knob of butter

a few slivers of Ibérico ham (or Serrano) each

a few anchovies (optional)

a sprinkle of chilli flakes (Aleppo chilli is particularly good)

Get a frying pan on to a high heat, drizzle in the olive oil and when it begins to shimmer, chuck in the Padrón. They will spit and splutter, but fear not, cook until they are blistered all over and starting to soften. Then pour into a Tupperware box, season with salt and squeeze over the juice of half a lemon, give it a shake and put the lid on (this also works in a bowl with a plate on top). This should keep them warm while you crack on with the eggs.

Working quickly, crack the eggs into the pan, season with salt and pepper and put the toast on. When ready, butter the toast lavishly, lay on the ham, then the eggs and scatter over the Padrón. Finish with a few anchovies, if using, and a sprinkling of chilli flakes.

SMOKED HADDOCK *&* LEEK RAREBIT

WE GREW UP EATING MANY A WELSH RAREBIT AS KIDS, a firm favourite for lunch on a drizzly autumnal weekend. Bubbling cheese on toast gently spiced with cayenne and finished with lashings of Worcestershire sauce . . . what more could you want? This is a riff on the infamous classic, where you gently poach a fillet of smoked haddock in cream, before mixing with strong Cheddar and slow-cooked leeks. This is then spread on toast and crisped under the grill, until it bubbles and caramelises. On those cold days when the courgettes have finally given in to frost, the ground is hard but the veg garden beds need a lot of work, this is the kind of thing we make in the morning to keep us going all day.

SERVES 6

350g fillet of undyed smoked haddock

1 bay leaf

100ml whole milk

150ml double cream

400g leeks (about 2–3)

50g unsalted butter

200g quality mature Cheddar

2 tsp Dijon mustard

½ nutmeg

6 pieces of fresh white sourdough (or even a really good tin loaf)

Place the smoked haddock and bay leaf in a pan and pour over the milk and cream. You might need to cut the fish in two so that it fits snugly. Season well with salt and pepper and bring to a gentle simmer with the lid on for just a few minutes (5 max), until the haddock is flaking and just cooked. Pour the contents of the pan into a separate bowl.

Next, slice the leeks in half lengthways and then across into thin slices, wash in the sink to remove any grit, then chuck into the pan while still wet, along with the butter and a generous pinch of salt. Put the pan on a medium heat and cook the leeks with the lid on until they're sweet and tender, stirring every so often and making sure they don't brown, about 10–15 minutes. Meanwhile, peel the skin off the haddock and flake the fish into the cream, looking out for any bones. When the leeks are ready, pour this cream into the pan and give it a good mix. On a very low heat, grate in the Cheddar, add the mustard and grate in the nutmeg, mixing until the Cheddar melts. Have a taste and adjust the seasoning as necessary.

If using straight away . . . toast the bread until it is crisp on both sides and place on a baking tray lined with parchment. Generously spread the haddock mix over the toast, about 1–2cm thick and right up to the edges. Place under the grill until golden and bubbling. Serve immediately! Great on its own outside, but excellent with a cold Bloody Mary and a crisp peppery salad.

FASOLAKIA

THERE ARE MANY RECIPES AROUND THE MEDITERRANEAN for green beans cooked in olive oil and tomato sauce, each with its own regional twist. This is the traditional Greek version, called fasolakia, where the beans are slowly braised in tomato with a lot of olive oil until they take on this magical velvety texture. This is something I make a lot towards the end of summer to use the overwhelming supply of beans from the garden; once they get going, it's a plant that's hard to keep up with. If you can track down some yellow beans to go alongside the green, the colour looks particularly pretty. This is a great veggie main, served with a hunk of bread and finished with lots of feta and oregano, but also makes a fantastic side for barbecued lamb.

SERVES 4–6

125ml quality olive oil

1 large brown onion, finely chopped

5 cloves of garlic, finely sliced

2 red chillies, finely chopped (or a pinch of chilli flakes)

a few generous pinches of dried oregano, plus extra for serving

1 tbsp cumin seeds

2 x 400g tins plum tomatoes (or 700g fresh tomatoes), roughly chopped

500g waxy potatoes, cut into large wedges

500g green beans

200ml water

80g pitted Kalamata olives

1 tsp caster sugar, if needed

for serving

a pack or two of feta cheese

a hunk of bread

In a large pan, heat the olive oil and, once warm, add the onion with a decent pinch of salt. Fry for 10 minutes, stirring every so often, until soft but not browned. Then add the garlic, chillies, oregano and cumin seeds and fry for a few minutes until fragrant, being careful not to let the garlic take on any colour. Add the tomatoes and potatoes with a big pinch of salt, bring up to a simmer, and cook for 15 minutes with the lid on. Then add the beans, stirring them into the sauce. Cook for a further 20–30 minutes, until the potatoes are soft and the beans velvety. Add the water bit by bit if you feel the pan is drying out. Often recipes call for green beans to be crisp and crunchy, but this is not the case here – you want them to be very tender, so much so that you could cut them with the side of a fork or spoon.

When ready, turn off the heat and stir through the olives. Leave the pan to settle with the lid on for 15 minutes, then have a taste and adjust the seasoning as necessary. A teaspoon of sugar is sometimes needed to balance out the acidity of the tomato, and maybe a smack more chilli or salt – take your time to get the balance right. Serve warm, with a hunk of bread, a generous chunk of feta, lots of dried oregano and a healthy drizzle of your best olive oil.

SPINACH & RICOTTA GNUDI

NUDA MEANS NAKED IN ITALIAN, AND THAT IS JUST WHAT THESE LITTLE GNUDI ARE, the naked filling of ravioli barely held together by a semolina skin. Light as anything, it's the delicate texture that makes these special. I'd always been put off making them, as they need to sit in semolina overnight, but what a mistake that was – they're so easy to make and a joy to eat. Ideal as a light lunch or simple supper, but three of them make a great starter too. Just be careful when you toss them in the butter, as they are fragile and easily dented.

SERVES 3 AS A LIGHT
LUNCH, 6 AS A STARTER

250g ricotta, drained

200g spinach

1 clove of garlic

2 tbsp olive oil

*40g parmesan, plus extra
  for serving*

1 unwaxed lemon

250g fine semolina

to finish

100g unsalted butter

*a bunch of fresh sage,
  leaves picked*

⅓ nutmeg

Drained ricotta is best for making gnudi – it comes in a little net and is dryer than the usual stuff. If using normal ricotta, just pour it into a sieve and leave to drip for a while to remove excess moisture.

Wash the spinach to remove any grit and leave in a colander to drain. Crush the garlic with your palm and peel the skin, then roughly chop. Chuck the garlic into a large pan, pour over a glug of olive oil and place on a medium heat. Allow the garlic to slowly sizzle and perfume the oil, but before it takes on any colour, add the washed spinach. Season with salt and stir the spinach until it wilts, then pour into a sieve and leave to cool.

When the spinach has cooled enough to handle, squeeze out as much water as you can. Then place it in a tea towel, wrap it up and twist tightly to remove as much water as possible – this makes a vast difference later on. When dry, pour the spinach on to a chopping board and finely chop.

I like to use a food processor for this next step, but you can easily chop the spinach and whip the ricotta by hand if preferred. Put the drained ricotta into your food processor and blitz until smooth. Then grate in the parmesan and lemon zest, season with salt, add the spinach and blitz again to thoroughly combine. Have a taste and adjust the seasoning as necessary, making sure that the flavour pops.

CONTINUED OVERLEAF

Then scoop into a bowl and leave covered in the fridge to cool, as this makes it easier to roll into balls.

When the gnudi mix has cooled, scatter half of the semolina into a small tray or Tupperware box. Wet your hands ever so slightly, then take a tablespoon of the gnudi mix, roll it into a neat ball between your palms and gently place in the semolina. Repeat until you have rolled all the balls – I found this makes 18 balls; keeping your hands wet will help stop the mix sticking. Now scatter over the remaining semolina and gently shake the gnudi to cover and nestle them deep in the semolina. This will continue to dry them out, but also forms a skin that holds them together when cooking. Leave in the fridge overnight.

When ready to cook, get a pan of water on to a rolling boil and season well with salt. It should taste as salty as the sea. In a separate pan, melt the butter over a medium heat. Add the sage leaves and leave to sizzle for a minute or so to infuse the butter, then turn off the heat. At this point drop the gnudi into the boiling water; when they float, remove with a slotted spoon and add to the sage butter with a splash of the starchy water. Toss gently to coat in the butter, then serve the gnudi with lots of the butter, a few drops of lemon juice and a smattering of nutmeg and parmesan.

FISH COOKED IN A SPICED TOMATO SAUCE
with tahini & coriander

THIS IS BASED ON A FANTASTIC NORTH AFRICAN DISH CALLED CHRAIME. Fillets of white fish are gently cooked in a tangy tomato sauce spiced with paprika, cumin and preserved lemon, before being drizzled with tahini and torn coriander – it's divine. Cooking fish in this way yields beautifully tender flakes, which absorb tons of flavour from the tomato sauce with its lovely warming spices, ideal for when the weather begins to turn. Preserved lemon is a pretty key element here, adding both salinity and a tanginess, but it can be salty, so be careful with your seasoning. I often eat this on its own as a light supper, but it is great with couscous and pitta. The sauce can be made in advance, but I would save cooking the fish until you're going to eat it. Any white fish works well, either fillets or cut across the bone. (*Pictured overleaf.*)

SERVES 4

4 tbsp olive oil

1 brown onion, finely sliced

5 cloves of garlic, finely sliced

2 tbsp smoked paprika

1 tsp ground cumin (ideally toast 1 tbsp of seeds and then grind in a pestle and mortar)

a pinch of chilli flakes (or a few whole dried chillies)

2 tbsp tomato purée

2 x 400g tins of plum tomatoes

1–2 preserved lemons, depending on size

4 fillets or slices of white fish (hake, pollack, halibut, bass, etc.)

chopped fresh coriander (or parsley), for serving

CONT. OVERLEAF

In a wide pan, warm the olive oil, then add the onion with a pinch of salt and fry until soft. Add the garlic and spices and fry for a minute or two until fragrant, then add the tomato purée. Cook out the purée for a couple of minutes, stirring to make sure it doesn't catch on the bottom of the pan. Pour in the tinned tomatoes, then rinse out each tin with a splash of water and pour that in too. Break up the tomatoes with a wooden spoon and simmer for about 10–15 minutes to thicken the sauce. Quarter and deseed the preserved lemons, then chop into small pieces before adding to the sauce. I would recommend adding the lemon a tablespoon at a time, tasting as you go to find the right balance. I say this because they come in many sizes and strengths, so you really need to taste and get the amount right for you.

To make the tahini sauce, grate the garlic into a bowl, squeeze over the juice of half a lemon, mix together and leave for 5 minutes. The acidity of the lemon will relax the heat of the garlic. Pour in the tahini and whisk together – it will begin to stiffen – then slowly pour in the ice-cold water, a tablespoon at a time, whisking as you go until you have a smooth, drizzly sauce. You want it to be quite runny.

CONTINUED OVERLEAF

for the tahini sauce
1 clove of garlic
½ lemon
80g quality tahini
5–6 tbsp ice-cold water
a little ground cumin

Season with a pinch of salt and a dash of cumin. Taste and adjust with a little more salt and/or lemon as need be.

Season the fish and nestle it into the tomato sauce. Cook for about 5–10 minutes, depending on the thickness of the fillets, until *just* cooked. Serve immediately, with warm pitta and couscous, and finish with lots of tahini sauce and fresh coriander.

PAN-FRIED TROUT
with buttery mash & a velvety spinach sauce

THIS IS SUCH A SOOTHING DISH – fatty and delicate trout with its yielding and flaky texture on a bed of buttery mash, swimming in a bowl of velvety spinach and watercress sauce. Quite like something you'd eat on the *Titanic* but comforting and elegant in its simplicity. Perfect for those grey days in November when the rain is unrelenting and the wind ruthlessly persistent. It's a dish inspired by chef Jeremy Lee, and that arose out of my love for spinach soup, but on a cold day needing something more substantial, with a fillet of fish in the fridge and some leftover mash on the hob . . . this dish was born and is now a regular at home.

SERVES 4

4 fillets of trout

20g finely chopped fresh chives

for the spinach sauce

30g unsalted butter

olive oil

1 large brown onion, finely sliced

3 cloves of garlic, finely sliced

220–250g spinach (depending on the size of your bag)

150ml double cream

80g watercress

1 unwaxed lemon

for the mash

5 large baking potatoes

75g salted butter

100ml whole milk

1–2 tsp Dijon mustard

Start by making the spinach sauce. Chuck the butter in a heavy-based pan with a splash of olive oil over a medium heat. Once foaming, add the onion, garlic and a good pinch of salt. Fry for 10–15 minutes, until sweet and tender but not browned. Then add the spinach and briefly cook until wilted. Pour this all into a blender along with the cream and blitz until incredibly smooth. Now add the watercress in stages, blitzing as you go to find the right balance, using it raw much like a herb to add peppery punch. Grate in a touch of lemon zest, add a hefty crack of pepper and season with a pinch of salt, then blitz again. It's crying out for a squeeze of lemon, but do this right before you serve or the acidity will turn the vibrant green to a muddy brown. Place in the fridge and leave to cool.

Make a simple mash – I don't need to instruct you on this, but peel a good fluffy variety of potato, cut evenly and boil in generously salted water from cold so they cook evenly. Make sure they're cooked through but not falling apart, then strain and leave to steam. Mash with a ricer, push through a sieve or mash by hand. Melt the butter in a small pan with the milk, then add to the mash little by little to find the right consistency. Finish with mustard and salt to taste.

Pat the fish dry with kitchen paper. Season the fillets, then rub the skin with a touch of oil. Put a large frying pan on a medium-high heat – you don't want the pan to be smoking. Place the fish skin side down, pressing each

fillet into the pan. Fry until the skin is crisp – then it should easily release from the pan so that you can gently turn the fillets over and briefly fry on the other side until just cooked through in the middle. While doing this, warm the sauce in a small pan, ensure the mash is hot and season the spinach with a squeeze of lemon just before you're ready to serve. Pour the spinach sauce into bowls, top with the mash and then the fish, followed by a sprinkling of fresh chives.

TOMATO CURRY

BY EARLY SEPTEMBER THE TOMATOES ARE GROWING FASTER THAN WE CAN EAT THEM, and seeing as we planted them way back in February this is a just reward after months of tender care. You can't leave them on the vine too long or they quite literally burst with juice, so we pick them by the basket load and they find their way into almost everything we eat. Great vats simmer on the stove with garlic and chilli, to be jarred and stored for a bit of colour in winter. We roast them, ferment them, eat endless salads and have them on toast every day for breakfast. But this curry reigns supreme as the most delicious way to make a dent in the basket. Here, tomatoes are the star of the show – they get roasted whole with olive oil and salt in their various shapes and colours, until the flavours intensify and the juices run, before being plunged into a fragrant coconut curry and served with brown rice and fresh coriander. (*Pictured overleaf*.)

SERVES 6

5 star anise

10 cardamom pods

1 heaped tsp cumin seeds

1 heaped tsp coriander seeds

1kg quality tomatoes, a nice mix of colours and sizes

3 tbsp olive oil

2 tbsp coconut oil (or vegetable oil)

a big sprig of fresh curry leaves (ideally, but if hard to find, 20 dried leaves also work)

1 large brown onion or 2 medium, finely sliced

5 cloves of garlic, finely sliced

1 or 2 red chillies (depending on your heat preference), finely sliced

There are two ways to go about toasting the spices for this dish. I love keeping them whole, which adds a real burst of flavour when you bite into them. So I have used the tempering method as outlined below. BUT if you're not a huge fan of chewing on a whole cardamom or coriander seed, you can toast the spices in a dry pan first, then grind them to a powder in a pestle and mortar or spice grinder. If doing this, halve the amount of cardamom and star anise, as they're much stronger when ground.

Preheat your oven to 200°C fan. Place all the tomatoes on a large tray lined with a sheet of baking parchment and drizzle generously with olive oil. Season well with salt and place in the oven for 45 minutes–1 hour. You want the tomatoes to concentrate in flavour and caramelise slightly, but hold their shape and not collapse.

Separately, in a large heavy-based pan, melt the coconut oil over a medium heat. Once shimmering, add the spices and fry for a minute to bring out their flavours. This method is tempering, a way of toasting spices. But you have to be very careful they don't burn. After a minute they should smell very fragrant, so add the curry leaves and let them sizzle for a few seconds, then chuck in the onion, garlic, chillies and ginger. Season with a generous pinch of

40g fresh ginger, peeled and finely chopped

2 x 400g tins of full-fat coconut milk

50ml natural yoghurt (or 2 tsp tamarind paste if you want to keep it vegan), plus extra as needed

for serving

brown rice, fresh coriander and fried curry leaves

salt and mix well. On a low heat, cook the onions right down until they are sweet and tender, being very careful they don't burn (about 15 minutes).

At this point, pour in the coconut milk, then rinse out each tin with a little splash of water and add that too. Simmer gently for about 40 minutes, until the sauce thickens, then turn off the heat. Put the yoghurt into a bowl and pour in a ladle of the curry. Mix well, then pour the yoghurt into the curry. This gets the yoghurt used to the heat and stops it curdling when it hits the hot curry. This is a good time to have a taste and adjust the seasoning.

Now gently add the tomatoes and carefully fold them into the curry so as not to break them apart. Taste again, adding a bit more yoghurt if you want it a touch more sour, and more chilli if it needs more heat. Serve immediately – I think this is particularly good on brown rice, with lots of fresh coriander and some fried crispy curry leaves if you're putting on a show.

TOMATO & ROSEMARY FOCACCIA

ON MY FIRST DAY WORKING AT NOBLE ROT THEY TAUGHT ME how to make the bread and butter. It was a restaurant famed for its bread plate, so this was quite the responsibility. Star of the show was a springy focaccia with onion and rosemary, alongside a richly molassed soda bread and sourdough from Coombeshead Farm with salty butter whipped from French crème fraîche. Having never made bread or butter before, this was thrilling to learn, and from that day forwards, I made focaccia and soda bread twice a day for the year that I worked there. I must have made nearly a thousand loaves, and even though I left the restaurant seven years ago, I still make that focaccia to this day. It's a wonderfully uncomplicated recipe compared to some of the three-day techniques I see today. Rich with olive oil, the edges crisp in the oven and the fluffy centre has a gentle sweetness and oomphy saltiness, particularly good for dipping and dunking.

At the restaurant we'd often serve it with romesco and burrata, or cod's roe and soft-boiled eggs. But in autumn, I particularly love it cooked with a handful of cherry tomatoes on top, alongside homemade pesto, whipped ricotta and a simple tomato salad.

MAKES 1 FOCACCIA

500ml water

1 sachet of instant yeast (or 40g fresh yeast)

30g caster sugar

700g strong white bread flour

20g sea salt, plus more for topping

lots of olive oil

300g of a variety of cherry tomatoes

a few sprigs of fresh rosemary

fennel seeds (optional)

CONT. OVERLEAF

You can either make and bake the bread on the same day, or make the dough in the evening and leave it to prove slowly overnight, ready to bake in the morning.

Pour the water into the bowl of a stand mixer, add the yeast and sugar, whisk together, then pour in the flour followed by the salt. Using the dough hook, knead on a medium speed for about 10 minutes, until the dough is elastic and shiny. You can, of course, do this in a bowl and knead by hand. Remove from the stand, pour in a glug of olive oil and release the bread from the sides. Cover the bowl with cling film or a damp tea towel and leave to prove until it has doubled in size. You can either leave it in the warmth of your kitchen to bake later on that day, or leave it to rise in the fridge overnight.

When it has doubled in size, pour a proper glug of olive oil into a baking tray about 35cm x 30cm and 5cm deep. The bread needs to almost fry in the oil, so use more than you think. Knock the air out of the dough and pour it into the baking tray. Spread it out with your fingers, being careful

CONTINUED OVERLEAF

for the whipped ricotta

2 pots of ricotta, 500g in
total

1 unwaxed lemon

for serving

a simple tomato salad

homemade pesto
(see page 308)

it doesn't tear, then leave to rise again in a warm place, until the dough fills the tray and is fluffy and bouncy.

Preheat your oven to 240°C fan. When ready to bake, halve the cherry tomatoes and carefully place on the risen dough, trying not to knock out any of the air. Stud with rosemary, drizzle with some olive oil and sprinkle over a generous amount of sea salt and the fennel seeds, if using. Place in the oven and bake for 15 minutes, then turn the heat down to 200°C fan for another 20–30 minutes. You're looking for bread that's beautifully caramelised all over, so you might need to rotate the loaf in order that it cooks evenly, and be careful it doesn't burn. When ready, remove from the oven and from the tin and leave to cool on a wire rack.

To make the whipped ricotta, empty both pots of ricotta into a large bowl, grate in the lemon zest and squeeze in half a lemon's worth of juice. Season with a generous pinch of sea salt and whip together until it's smooth and silky.

Serve the focaccia with the whipped ricotta, a simple tomato salad and some homemade pesto.

POTATO, PANCETTA & TALEGGIO GALETTE

IMAGINE IF DAUPHINOISE AND TARTIFLETTE HAD A BABY and it arrived in the form of a tart. This galette is just that. Thinly sliced potatoes, crème fraîche, thyme and garlic are layered with pancetta and Taleggio above a wonderfully flaky pastry. This gets slowly cooked in the oven until the cheese and pancetta melt and meld with the tender potatoes. Served hot with a crisp and zingy salad, it will send a revered hush around the table as you all dig in. It's also a tart that is unusually good cold, so even if it's just a few of you, make the full tart and enjoy the remaining slices for breakfast, as we often do. (*Pictured overleaf.*)

SERVES 6

800g waxy potatoes

2 large brown onions, finely sliced

50g butter

2 tbsp olive oil

1 clove of garlic, finely grated

3 tbsp crème fraîche

a bunch of fresh thyme, leaves picked

galette pastry (see page 310)

150–200g Taleggio, thinly sliced

150g thinly sliced pancetta

1 egg, beaten

1 tsp fennel seeds

sea salt

Peel the potatoes and slice very thinly with a mandolin. Place in a colander and give them a rinse under the tap to wash away the excess starch, then leave to drain.

Put the onions, butter and half the olive oil into a pan on a medium heat, season well with salt and cook slowly until they are sweet and tender, but be careful they don't brown. When ready, after 10–15 minutes, set aside to cool.

Once the potatoes are dry, transfer to a bowl along with the onions, garlic, crème fraîche, thyme, remaining olive oil, salt and pepper. Mix well by hand, separating out the slices and working the crème fraîche into every nook and cranny.

Preheat your oven to 220°C fan.

Roll out the pastry on a sheet of baking parchment with a little flour to stop it sticking. You're looking for a wide disk about 4–5mm thick. The trick to rolling pastry is to keep turning it in circles, and roll away from you. If you just go back and forth with the rolling pin, the middle tends to get too thin. Carefully pull the parchment and pastry on to a sufficiently large tray. Leaving a 6–8cm border around the edge that you can fold over later, start neatly piling on the potato mixture. Once you have an even layer, follow with roughly a quarter of the Taleggio and pancetta, then follow with another layer of potatoes. Repeat until you have used most if not all of the potatoes, making sure it is well-cohered together and the top is even. Finish with a few slices of Taleggio, then fold over the edges of the galette, creasing them together with your fingers so they hold. Brush the beaten egg over the pastry and sprinkle over the fennel seeds and a little sea salt.

Place in the oven and bake for 10 minutes, then turn the heat down to 180°C fan and cook for 50 minutes–1 hour, until the potatoes are properly tender when skewered with a knife. Remove from the oven and leave to cool for 5 minutes, then slice and enjoy. You really do want a good zingy green salad to go with this. Chicory, gem, cider vinegar, olive oil, etc. to cut through and balance the rich tart.

CHICKEN & RICOTTA MEATBALLS IN BROTH
with orzo, crème fraîche & dill

IN THE DARKER DAYS OF AUTUMN AS THE OMINOUS GLOOM OF WINTER DESCENDS, I often find myself yearning for a bowl of healing chicken soup. We make quite a few versions at home and it's rare there's not a pot of broth bubbling on the stove. Sometimes I boil a whole chicken with a load of veg, then strip off the meat and throw it back into the broth with a dollop of aïoli. Mum makes a great soup of blended chicken with a ton of tarragon, wonderfully nourishing to combat the lurgy. But here we have a much-loved classic, with the addition of these divine meatballs, which are zingy with lemon and rich with ricotta. They have the most delicate texture and are light and juicy as can be.

SERVES 6

for the meatballs

6 boneless, skinless chicken thighs

120g fresh breadcrumbs

150g ricotta

1 egg yolk

a generous bunch of fresh tarragon (15–20g), finely chopped

zest of 1 unwaxed lemon

10g flaky sea salt and a generous crack of pepper

olive oil, for frying

for the broth

1 large onion, finely chopped

3 celery sticks, finely sliced

3 carrots, halved lengthways and finely sliced

1.7 litres really good chicken stock (see page 306)

250g orzo

20g fresh dill, finely chopped

20g fresh parsley, finely chopped

crème fraîche, for serving

To make the meatballs, roughly chop the chicken, then place in a food processor and blitz to a paste. Add the rest of the meatball ingredients apart from the oil and blitz again until well combined. Take a small amount of the mixture and roll into a patty, then fry in a large, heavy-based pan with a splash of olive oil until golden on each side – this should only take a few minutes. Remove, leave to cool, then have a taste. This should give you an idea of the seasoning, so adjust the rest of the mixture as necessary. Once you have done so, roll the rest of the mixture into small meatballs. Fry in batches until golden on all sides, taking care not to overcrowd the pan and adding more oil as necessary. Set the meatballs aside on a large plate or tray while you cook the vegetables.

Using the chicken fat that has rendered from the meatballs, fry the onion with a pinch of salt for 10–12 minutes, until completely soft and sweet, taking care it doesn't brown. Add the celery and carrots, fry for a few minutes, then add the chicken stock. Put the lid on the pan and bring up to a simmer for about 10–15 minutes, until the veg is tender. Then add the meatballs and orzo and cook for another 6–8 minutes, until the pasta is al dente. Taste for seasoning, then stir through the herbs and serve in warm bowls with a dollop of crème fraîche.

EPIC TARRAGON ROAST CHICKEN

THERE ARE RECIPES IN THIS BOOK THAT I LOVE BECAUSE THEY ARE INTERESTING, there are those that I love for their simplicity, and there are those that I find myself making again and again. This is the latter, a great roast chicken, the heart of home cooking and one of life's great pleasures. I relish the ritual, my family's fight over the wings, the secret chef's treats of the oysters, the leftover sandwiches and bubbling stocks. There is no meal that makes me feel more at home. In my mind, there are three keys to a good roast chicken . . . juicy meat, brown salty skin and most importantly a ton of sauce. And it's the sauce of this chicken that really sets it apart: handfuls of tarragon, lashings of cream and a proper dollop of mustard, which when combined with the cooking juices, garlic and wine creates a truly epic mouthful.

SERVES 5

1 organic chicken

3 tbsp olive oil

1 whole head of garlic

250ml quality double cream

a 20g bunch of fresh tarragon, stalks removed, roughly chopped

1 large heaped tbsp Dijon mustard

a glass of dry white wine

Preheat your oven to 220°C fan and start by spatchcocking the chicken. To do this, turn it over and cut along one side of the spine from the tail to the neck. Then turn it over, open out the two sides and press down hard to flatten it. Your butcher will gladly do this for you. Lay the chicken in a large, high-sided roasting tray, season generously with salt on both sides and leave for an hour at room temperature so it loses the chill of the fridge.

When ready, generously drizzle the skin with olive oil and work it into all the nooks and crannies. Smash the head of garlic and hide the cloves underneath the chicken, then roast in the oven for 20–30 minutes, until the skin begins to turn golden brown. Meanwhile, mix the cream, tarragon and mustard in a bowl and season well with salt and pepper. After 20–30 minutes, turn the oven down to 140°C fan, take out the chicken and pour a generous glass of white wine into the tray. Then pour the tarragon cream all over the chicken and place back in the oven for 30–40 minutes until it's ready. To judge when it's cooked, I check the deepest part of the thigh with a temperature probe, looking for 65–70°C. If you don't have one, prod this point with a skewer and ensure the juices run clear. At this point, remove from the oven and leave to rest for 15 minutes, covered loosely with a bit of foil. Carve straight into the tray and serve as you like, with lots of the sauce, garlic and a zingy green salad.

LAMB GRILLED ON HERB SKEWERS
with marinated red peppers & garlic sauce

LAMB COOKED OVER FIRE IS A GREAT PLEASURE. There is such joy in the way the meat caramelises and the fat catches flavour, dripping on to the embers below and sending up whisps of fragrant smoke. Here the lamb is spiced and seasoned before being skewered on rosemary and bay branches. Cooked gently over coals while being brushed with butter, the herbs smoke in the heat and infuse the meat from within. Served with peppers cooked until soft and smoky, the flesh stripped from the skin and marinated with garlic, vinegar and capers. Then finished with fresh basil and warm focaccia to mop up the juices.

SERVES 4

2 whole heads of garlic

300ml whole milk

olive oil

500g lamb neck fillet

1 tbsp ground cumin

1 tsp smoked paprika

1 tsp Aleppo chilli

bay and rosemary skewers
 (but of course, normal
 kebab skewers work too)

a little butter

a handful of fresh basil

for the marinated peppers

12 peppers (a mix of red,
 yellow and sweet pointy
 piquillo peppers, if you
 can find them)

1 clove of garlic

2 tbsp sherry or light
 balsamic vinegar

3 tbsp quality olive oil

2 tbsp capers

a tin of salted anchovies,
 drained and roughly torn
 (optional)

Start by making the garlic sauce. Remove the skins from the two heads of garlic. I do this by placing the two bulbs in a bowl and covering with boiling water. Leave for a minute, then remove – the skin should now come away easily. Place the cloves in a small pan, cover with the milk and season with a pinch of salt. Cook on a low heat, being careful the milk doesn't catch, until the rawness of the garlic has softened. Depending on how punchy you like your garlic, this takes between 5 and 10 minutes. When ready, either use an immersion blender in the pan, or pour the contents into a blender and blitz until completely smooth. Pour in 2–3 tablespoons of olive oil, to thicken and enrich the sauce, then taste and adjust the seasoning.

Dice the lamb into bite-size chunks, place in a bowl, season well with salt and cover with the spices. Mix well and leave to marinate for 30 minutes. To make the skewers, if you're lucky enough to have a bay or rosemary bush at home, snip off 6–8 strong stalks. Strip the leaves from the branches and save them for another recipe, but leave a few leaves at the top of each skewer. At the bottom, use a knife to create a sharp point, then thread the lamb on to the skewers; if you don't have access to these herbs, you can of course use normal skewers. While the lamb is marinating, light a decent amount of quality charcoal – initially the heat

CONTINUED OVERLEAF

will be too great to cook the lamb, but you can use it to grill the peppers.

You need to grill the peppers until the skins burn and blister and the flesh collapses. Ideally, this is best done over the hot coals of a barbecue, but you can also cook the peppers directly over the flame of your gas hob, or blast them under the grill. Cook until they begin to soften and collapse, turning as you go, to char the skin all over, then place in a large bowl and cover with cling film or a plate. Here they will steam and continue cooking, which releases the skin from the flesh and makes them easy to peel. Leave for 20 minutes, then peel the skins off the peppers and remove the stems and seeds. By the end you should have lots of sweet, smoky peppers and a puddle of their juice in the bowl. Treat this liquid as the beginnings of a salad dressing. Grate in the garlic, slosh in the vinegar and season well with salt. Now pour this over the peppers, drizzle over the olive oil and mix well. Add the capers and anchovies, if using, and leave to marinate while you cook the lamb.

By now, the heat of the charcoal should have died down a bit. Keep an eye on the fire, adding a little more charcoal if you think it needs it, but the lamb doesn't need much heat. Place the skewers on the grill and don't touch them – they should slowly begin to sizzle and char. Once you can see they've taken on some colour, turn and brown the other side. At this point, brush a little butter over them as they cook – don't overdo it or it will drip and catch fire, but a little butter adds a lovely richness later on. When they are caramelised but still feel a little springy and tender, remove them from the heat and leave to rest for a few minutes. Plate up the peppers alongside a puddle of the garlic sauce, then top with the lamb and finish with lots of basil.

SLOW-ROAST CRISPY PORK BELLY

A SLOW-ROASTED, CRISPY-SKINNED PORK BELLY is one of the finest mouthfuls there is. Rich in flavour with a melt-in-the-mouth texture and crunchy crackling, it is a truly exceptional roast. Here are the tools to achieve beautifully crisp crackling and the juiciest meat – you do need to start the recipe the night before, but it is the drying overnight in the fridge that achieves that heavenly salty crunch.

The reason a piece of pork belly is such a great cut for slow roasting are the layers of fat interspersed through the meat, which melt during the cooking process and keep things ludicrously succulent and tender. Putting vegetables below allows them to cook in those dripping porky juices while also infusing their flavour into the meat above. Here I've used a medley of tart cooking apples, thyme and onion, which melt and caramelise in the fat, providing a rustic sauce with an acidity that perfectly cuts through the richness of the meat. I love this with a generous spoon of mustard mash and some lemony purple sprouting broccoli, but enjoy with any of your favourite sides. (*Pictured overleaf.*)

SERVES 6

1.5kg pork belly, skin on
2–3 cooking apples
3 large brown onions
a few sprigs of fresh thyme
a glass of cider or white wine

for the marinade
1½ tbsp sea salt
1 tbsp fennel seeds
1 tbsp dried oregano
1 tbsp dried thyme

Place the pork on a wire rack in the sink. Boil a full kettle, then pour the boiling water over the pork skin – this scalds the pork and tightens the skin, which helps create amazing crackling. Pat dry with a tea towel, then with a craft knife, or a similarly sharp paring knife or razor, score the pork skin from edge to edge in lines 1cm apart. Don't be tempted to do diagonals, as this causes the crackling to break when carving. The aim here is to carefully score the skin down to the fat below, but do not go through to the meat, otherwise liquid will escape from the meat when cooking and ruin the crispness of the crackling. It is surprisingly tricky scoring the skin well without piercing through to the meat, so take your time. You can usually ask your butcher to do this for you.

In a pestle and mortar, roughly bash the ingredients for the marinade together, then rub this all over the underside and sides of the pork, but leave the skin unsalted. Make sure the skin is properly dry, then place on a large plate or tray in

CONTINUED OVERLEAF

the fridge overnight, with room for the pork to breathe. This will dry out the skin ahead of cooking the next day.

The next day, remove the pork from the fridge and preheat your oven to 240°C fan – as high as it'll go, essentially. Place the pork on a baking tray lined with baking parchment and pat the skin dry one last time before generously seasoning with flaky salt. You want to really massage it into all those nooks and crannies created by the scoring. Put the tray in the middle of your oven and roast for 45 minutes–1 hour, until the skin is puffed and crackling, but keep a careful eye, rotating the tray if needs be and ensuring that it doesn't burn. Remove from the oven and turn the heat right down to 160°C fan.

Peel the apples and cut into quarters, then remove the cores. Halve the onions, remove the skins and again cut into quarters or even eighths. Lift up the pork and evenly spread the apples, onions and thyme sprigs in the tray, season well and stir through the juices, then pour in the cider and place the pork back on top. Put the tray back in the oven at 160°C fan for 2½ hours, by which time the pork should be supremely tender, the skin crisp and the apple and onion molten and tender.

Turn the oven off, open the door and leave the pork in there to stay warm while it rests for 15 minutes. Spend this time getting your sides piping hot. Then remove the pork, slice and serve with lots of the lovely apple and onion.

STEWED PLUMS, WHIPPED YOGHURT, MINT & GRANOLA

IN SEPTEMBER THE PLUM TREE BY THE VEG PATCH HANGS HEAVY WITH FRUIT, its branches laden like a strained washing line on the brink of collapse. How this small tree produces such bountiful abundance each year bemuses me; often a branch or two fracture under the weight of fruit. We pick them by the basket, teetering on a rickety ladder and battling the wasps, to make jams, gins, chutneys and all sorts.

This recipe is a particular favourite that is just as good for breakfast as it is after a sunny September lunch. I got the idea for the yoghurt folded with whipped cream and honey from the pastry chef Nicola Lamb – it's a wonderful twist that gives it a lighter and more elegant touch, but I often use labneh instead.

SERVES 6

80g quality granola or pistachios

30g butter

6–10 plums, depending on size, halved and destoned

20g golden caster sugar

60ml Madeira, brandy or sweet sherry

280ml double cream

1–2 tbsp runny honey

350ml natural yoghurt

a couple of sprigs of fresh mint

Preheat your oven to 160°C fan. If using pistachios, pour them into a tray or ovenproof pan and cook for about 10–15 minutes max, until they are toasted and crunchy but not burnt. Set a timer – I always forget.

Put a wide frying pan on a medium-high heat and add the butter. When it begins to foam, swirl it around, then add the plums, cut side down. Ideally, they should fill the pan. Sprinkle over the sugar and let it gently sizzle so that the plums release their juice, then pour in the Madeira. A lovely thick and unctuous sauce should slowly be created. Before the plums get too soft, turn them over to cook the other side. The ideal is to end up with a beautiful sauce and plums that still hold their shape but are soft and delicious. So don't cook them for too long, and add a splash of water if the sauce gets too thick. You need enough for each person to get a spoonful.

While the plums are cooking, pour the cream into a large bowl. Whip it until it is light and voluptuous but still has a nice movement to it. Whipping cream perfectly is an art, taking it far enough to create that luxurious feel, but not so far that it begins to solidify. When ready, drizzle in 1 tablespoon of honey and add the yoghurt. Gently fold together and have a taste; you can add a touch more honey if you like, but don't overdo it.

Finally, crush the toasted pistachios, if using, and roughly chop the mint leaves. Spoon a generous dollop of the cream into a bowl and make a crater in the middle. Add two or three warm plum halves and a spoon of the sauce, then top with the granola or pistachios and mint.

You can make a lot of this ahead; just slightly underdo the plums so that you can warm them up again without overcooking them. But the active ingredients in the yoghurt will begin to work on the cream if left too long, so I would recommend making that more or less in the moment.

RIPPLED BERRY PARFAIT

MUCH LIKE AN ITALIAN SEMIFREDDO (see page 161), a parfait is also a frozen mousse, with a pleasing texture somewhere between ice cream and marshmallow. But where the semifreddo relies on whipping egg whites to create trapped air, the French parfait uses a fun technique called pâte à bombe to whip air into the yolks.

The best thing about this parfait is that you can use the recipe throughout the year with all sorts of seasonal berries. This one is made with wild blackberries and mulberries from our tree, but blackcurrants are particularly good, as are elderberries, raspberries, damsons, peaches and even sour cherries. Whatever fruit you use, the key is that you cook the compote right down until it's jammy and syrupy – this ensures it won't crystallise when you freeze it.

SERVES 8–10

5 egg yolks

20ml water

30ml honey

75g caster sugar

350ml double cream

1 tsp vanilla extract

for the compote

300g berries (see intro)

150g caster sugar

1–2 lemons (depending on the sharpness of the fruit you're using)

Start by lining a 25cm x 10cm terrine mould or loaf tin with two or three sheets of cling film, leaving enough excess hanging over the sides to help you pull out the parfait later.

To make the compote, put the berries and sugar into a saucepan, place on a medium heat and cook until the sugar melts and the berries release their juice. Continue to simmer until the sauce thickens and becomes syrupy, ideally making sure the temperature reaches 103°C. This ensures that you have cooked off enough water, which prevents it forming crystals when it freezes. When ready, remove from the heat and add a dash of lemon juice. Mix and taste – you want sweetness with a sharp kick, so add more lemon if it needs it to get the balance right. I like to keep the texture quite chunky but you can make it as rough or smooth as you like. Leave the compote to cool before carrying on with the rest of the recipe.

Now for the fun bit. I like to do this in a stand mixer, but you can also do it by hand with an electric whisk. Place the egg yolks in the bowl of a stand mixer. Pour the water, honey and caster sugar into a small pan on a high heat and bring to the boil. Cook until the syrup reaches 118°C, which ensures that the perfect amount of water has evaporated off. While the syrup is boiling, turn on the mixer and whip those yolks until they're pale and fluffy. The minute the syrup

CONTINUED OVERLEAF

reaches 118°C, turn the mixer right down (you don't want hot syrup flicking into your eye, been there, not fun) and with the machine running slowly, trickle the syrup down the side of the bowl into the yolks. When it's all in, crank up the speed and whip until the bottom of the bowl is cool to the touch and the yolks are thick and glossy with a pale caramel colour. This takes about 6 minutes; the technique is called pâte à bombe and is the beginning of many mousse recipes.

While the machine is running, pour the cream into a separate bowl, add the vanilla and whip together. You are looking for that perfect whipped cream texture: smooth, light and airy. Be careful not to take it too far – if too firm it doesn't fold as well into the mixture, so think light and airy but still a little loose. Ideally, whip by hand so that you can feel the texture change, in a back and forth W-shaped motion, not in circles. When the cream's ready, the yolks should be too. Add a third of the yolks to the cream and gently fold together by hand, aiming to retain as much air as possible. Then gently fold in the next third, followed by the last. Now *very* carefully fold in the berry compote, leaving lovely dark ripples. Don't overmix, but make sure the compote is evenly distributed. Gently pour the mixture into your prepared mould, fold over the cling film sides and place in the freezer immediately. Leave until firm and set. You're looking for it to be frozen through, but not rock solid. If it has gone a little too hard, leave it on the plates for a bit once sliced until the texture is perfect.

When ready to serve, remove the top layer of cling film, place a chopping board on top of the mould and flip. Hopefully it should slide out easily with a little tap, but if it doesn't, gently tug on the cling film and pull it out. Quickly slice and serve – it's divine but fast melting. Wrap up any leftovers and immediately freeze for another day.

DAMSON FRANGIPANE TART

A GOOD FRANGIPANE TART IS ONE OF THE MOST USEFUL RECIPES OF THEM ALL, up there with crumble as one of the great ways to enjoy seasonal fruit throughout the year. It's a pretty dish that can be made the day before, feeds many and is ideal for dinner parties or events. I've used damsons here, as they were growing in the garden, but you can take this as a base recipe and use any fruit you like. Rhubarb works well in winter, apricots or gooseberries in spring, raspberries, blackcurrants and cherries in summer, plums, pears and apples in autumn, even dark chocolate and marmalade in the darkest depths of January.

Making my own pastry was not something I did often before working in restaurants, so I completely understand if you lean towards shop-bought, but once you learn how, it is actually incredibly easy. (*Pictured overleaf.*)

SERVES 8

for the shortcrust pastry
200g plain flour
100g very cold unsalted butter, cubed
a small glass of ice-cold water

for the frangipane
250g blanched whole almonds
250g unsalted butter, softened
200g caster sugar
zest of 1 unwaxed lemon (or orange, depending on the fruit)
2 eggs
2 tbsp self-raising flour (optional)
500g damsons, pitted

for serving
double cream or crème fraîche

Make your pastry as per the recipe on page 309. As the pastry chills, make the frangipane. Put the blanched almonds into the food processor (no need to rinse it after making the pastry), blitz to a fine crumb, then tip into a bowl. Now add the butter, sugar and lemon zest to the food processor and blitz until the butter goes pale and fluffy. Whisk the eggs together, then, with the processor running, very slowly trickle into the whipped butter. If you go too fast it will curdle. I like to add 2 tablespoons of self-raising flour at this point, which adds a lovely lightness to the texture later on. Put the almonds back in and blitz again to combine. Scrape into a bowl and chill in the fridge while you blind-bake the pastry.

Preheat your oven to 170°C fan. On a lightly floured surface, roll the pastry out to about 3mm thick. Lift into a 25cm fluted tart case with a removable bottom, and gently press the pastry into the tin, leaving an overhang around the sides. Prick the pastry base all over with a fork and chill in the freezer for 20 minutes. Then line the pastry with baking parchment and fill with baking beans. Put the tin on to a baking tray and bake for 15–20 minutes, until the pastry is

CONTINUED OVERLEAF

firm, then remove the beans and parchment and return to the oven for another 10 minutes, until golden. Trim off any excess pastry with a serrated knife.

Roughly dollop the frangipane into the pastry and top with the damsons (you may not need all of them, but bear in mind that you want to have a damson in most mouthfuls, so be generous) and gently press into the frangipane. Place in the oven and immediately turn the temperature down to 160°C fan. Bake for 1 hour 10 minutes, until the frangipane is golden and set. Remove from the oven and allow to cool in the tin for about 15 minutes before slicing. Serve with cream or crème fraîche.

DARK CHOCOLATE, OAT
& HAZELNUT COOKIES

THERE'S ONLY SO MUCH YOU CAN SAY ABOUT A COOKIE, but one thing I do know is that it's pretty hard to resist the heavenly smell as they bake. This is quite a grown-up recipe, not too sweet, with a generous amount of dark chocolate and quite a savoury undertone from the oats and toasted hazelnuts. I like them warm from the oven, finished with a sprinkle of salt over the dark molten chocolate, but they are just as good left to cool when they take on a pleasing crunch. The joy of this recipe is that once the dough is made, they live in a box in the freezer and can be baked straight from frozen whenever you like.

MAKES 14

60g blanched hazelnuts

150g unsalted butter,
  softened

120g soft brown sugar

60g caster sugar

1 egg, beaten

1 tsp vanilla extract

½ tsp flaky sea salt

40g oats

180g self-raising flour

125g dark chocolate, 70%

Preheat your oven to 180°C fan. Place the hazelnuts on a tray and toast in the oven for about 10 minutes, until they're slightly golden and have a lovely nutty crunch. Leave to cool, then roughly bash into smaller pieces – don't go too fine. Next, cream the butter with the two sugars. I use a stand mixer with the paddle attachment, but a deep bowl and hand whisk work well too. You want the butter to go pale and fluffy, so it's aerated by the sugar. But be careful not to overwhisk the butter, as this will adversely affect the cookies later on; it should only take 2–3 minutes tops. Scrape down the sides of the bowl to make sure the sugar is evenly incorporated.

In a small bowl, whisk the egg with the vanilla extract, then with the mixer running, pour the egg into the butter a little at a time until incorporated. Turn the mixer off, and add the salt, oats and flour. Turn back on and mix into a cohesive dough, again scraping down the sides a few times as it mixes. While the chocolate is still in its packet, smash it a few times against the work surface to break it up, then pour on to a chopping board and chop into large chips with a sharp knife. Add the chocolate and nuts to the dough and fold in by hand with a spatula.

Roll the dough into 60g balls and place in a Tupperware box in the freezer, with baking parchment between the layers if you're stacking. I keep them like this and bake one or two at a time straight from frozen when needed, as I like them warm and molten from the oven.

Place on a tray with a sheet of baking parchment and bake at 180°C fan for between 13 and 15 minutes – this really depends on whether you like a slightly gooey middle, or a crisper cookie. Remove from the oven and leave to sit for another 5 minutes while they continue to set before tucking in. Sprinkle with a generous touch of flaky salt and enjoy!

PLUM & FIG LEAF JAM

IT'S FUNNY, I'M NOT SOMEONE WHO EATS MUCH JAM, being more of an egg person at breakfast, but I do love making it. We have a shed next to the chicken coop, home to a million spiders and filled to the brim with row upon row of jams, marmalade, honey, chutneys and boozy infusions. There's something so meditative and peaceful about jamming, that connection to the seasons through bubbling cauldrons of fruit and sugar, made from baskets dripping with wild berries brought home by stained fingers. Of all the jams I make, this is the one that reigns supreme, and since moving to Dorset, where we have an incredibly generous plum tree, I've made it every year. Plums make a great jam with or without the fig leaves, the fruit collapsing into an oozing texture, with a welcome tartness and vibrant colour. But the addition of fig leaves is really quite special. They have a floral, almost buttery and almondy aroma, the flavour of which goes beautifully with the plums.

A note on sugar: when I'm making jam, I use a ratio of 1kg of fruit to 350–500g of pectin or jamming sugar. This is less than half the amount of sugar a traditional jam recipe would use and I find that means you can taste the fruit much better. The key, though, is that you have to use jamming sugar for the added pectin to set the jam. Use this formula as a base for whatever seasonal fruit you have to hand. With damsons, which are very sour, you'll need to use the full 500g of sugar, but with peaches, figs, plums, etc., which are much sweeter, go for 350g.

Jams are great to play around with – try adding a few cardamom pods, star anise, fig leaves (as here), a mix of berries and fruits, different citrus, zests and even nuts. Treat them playfully as you do savoury food, and then TASTE to get the balance right. If you want to add a touch more lemon juice, go ahead; more sugar . . . go ahead.

Sugar is a key part of the preservation qualities in jam. Because I've reduced the amount so much, you really do need to sterilise your jars to ensure they keep forever. Once opened, keep an eye on them and if any mould appears, scrape it off and store the jar in the fridge. (*Pictured overleaf.*)

2kg Victoria plums,
  destoned and cut into
  quarters
2 fig leaves
300ml water
700g pectin or jamming
  sugar
2 lemons

Put the plums, fig leaves and water into a large heavy-based pan. Bring up to a gentle simmer and cook for about 15 minutes, until the skins and flesh have softened, but not entirely collapsed. Turn the heat right down, then pour in the sugar and squeeze in the lemon juice. Gently simmer and mix well until the sugar melts, then ramp up the heat and cook for about 20–30 minutes, stirring often, until the jam thickens and hits a temperature of 102°C. To test, put a plate in the freezer and when you think the jam is ready, quickly put a small spoon's worth on the frozen plate and leave it to cool for a minute. Then run your finger through the jam in a line and if the two sides hold and don't immediately come back together, that's thick enough for me. I prefer a lighter, more nuanced flavoured jam over one that's gone dark from cooking until the ideal setting point.

To sterilise your jars, run them through a very hot dishwasher cycle. Or place them in a tray, then fill the jars and cover the lids with boiling water from the kettle. Leave for 5 minutes, then pour out the water and put briefly into a 100°C fan oven to dry completely.

Pour the jam into the jars, ideally using a funnel – but don't fill them right to the top. Place on the lids and invert the jars. Leave them upside down for 20 minutes, then turn over and leave to cool. Label and store in a cool, dark place until you're ready to tuck in!

PICKLED CUCUMBERS

TOWARDS THE END OF AUTUMN THE VEG PATCH IS OVERFLOWING but time is running out. We fill wheelbarrows of marrows, pick endless tomatoes, fill bags of basil and hang up strings of chillies and onions to dry, trying to make the most of our produce before the season ends. The thing about growing your own is that you can't control when something's going to be ready. You can plant successionally, which means planting small batches often, to try and create a steady supply rather than gluts, but when a plant is in its prime there's nothing you can do to keep up with it. This is where the fun of preservation comes in! In winter none of these exciting things grow, but through preservation I can extend the season and enjoy colourful summer veg through the leaner months. We do a lot of fermentation, drying, canning, and of course pickling.

The difference between a homemade pickle and a shop-bought one is vast. I love a gherkin, but so often the vinegar used is throat-strippingly strong and there's no nuance in the flavour whatsoever. Making a pickle at home couldn't be easier, and allows you to preserve veg in its prime with delicious additional flavours. They make a great snack alongside bread and butter, or with a hunk of cheese, even in a sandwich. Here is my generic pickle recipe with lots of lovely additional flavours that you can use to pickle anything really . . . beetroots, cauliflower, carrots, French beans, turnips, radishes, you name it. The only thing you need to adapt is how you prep the veg. Most things can be pickled raw. But let's take beetroot, for example: if pickling raw, I would peel and cut them into thin slices; if pickling larger chunks, I would boil the beetroot until tender, then cut into chunks and pickle. Cauliflower I would cook very briefly first, making sure to retain a lot of texture; carrots, radishes etc. I pickle whole.

This recipe is based on a classic 3:2:1 pickle – 3 parts vinegar, 2 parts water and 1 part sugar. BUT the strength of vinegars varies so much these days, and I often find I need additional sugar to balance this out. As with all cooking, just have a taste and add more sugar if you think it needs it. But also seek out a high-quality vinegar that isn't too harsh on the throat. Once you've got the hang of pickling, play around with different spices and vinegars – there's a whole world to explore out there.

MAKES 1 LARGE JAR

2 cucumbers, sliced into
 jaunty chunks
1 tbsp salt
500ml cider vinegar
250ml water
125g caster sugar
¼ tsp ground turmeric
6 black peppercorns
2 bay leaves
1 brown onion, thinly sliced
1 tbsp fennel seeds
1 tbsp brown mustard seeds
½ tsp chilli flakes
3 tbsp olive oil

Start by mixing the cucumbers with the salt. Leave for 1–2 hours, or overnight if you have the time, until the cucumbers have released some of their liquid, then drain this off.

While the cucumbers are draining, move on to making the pickling liquid. In a medium pan, gently heat the vinegar, water, sugar, turmeric, black peppercorns and bay leaves until the sugar has completely dissolved. Then turn up the heat and allow the mixture to boil for a further 5 minutes.

During this time, add the sliced onion, fennel seeds, mustard seeds and chilli flakes to the cucumbers and give them a good mix, until they are evenly coated with the spices and onion.

Put the cucumbers into a 1 litre Kilner jar and cover with the pickling liquid. Add the olive oil to create a seal and leave to cool. Cover with a little parchment paper, close the jar and store in a cool, dark place for at least a day before tucking in.

These last a long time, but do degrade with age. Keep cool in the warmer months to extend their life.

THE SAUCE

THIS SITS SOMEWHERE BETWEEN KETCHUP AND BROWN SAUCE but, dare I say, it's better than both. Sweet, tangy and wonderfully spiced, there's nothing I'd rather have in a sausage sandwich or bacon butty. A slug of this will take any breakfast to the next level, but it's also great on the barbecue, both as a marinade and as a glaze. Once made it never goes off and gets better with age. I make great vats each year in autumn with the last of our tomatoes and the first apples – it is an elixir and my shelf would be desperately sad without it.

MAKES ABOUT 5 LARGE
JAM JARS

3 brown onions, diced

4 tbsp olive oil

*3 fresh chillies, deseeded
and finely chopped*

3 tsp ground cloves

2 tsp ground allspice

*1 large head of garlic, cloves
grated or smashed*

*5cm thumb of fresh ginger,
peeled and roughly
chopped*

*3.5kg plum tomatoes,
roughly chopped*

*3 cooking apples, roughly
chopped*

100g flaky salt

650g caster sugar

300g soft brown sugar

*650ml organic red wine
vinegar*

You need your largest pan. Start by gently frying the onions in the olive oil for 15 minutes, until sweet and tender. Then add the chillies, spices, garlic and ginger. Fry gently for 3 minutes to activate the aromatics, then follow with the rest of the ingredients. This now needs to quietly simmer for 3 hours. Keep an eye, stirring when needed, and be careful it doesn't catch on the bottom of the pan.

When ready, blend with an immersion blender until smooth, then pass through a mouli. If you don't have one, push the sauce through a sieve with a wooden spoon or spatula. Have a taste and check the seasoning – you might like to add a touch more sugar, a splash of vinegar or even a pinch of chilli flakes or hot sauce for a gentle kick. If still a little runny for your liking, you can reduce this further.

To store, I usually run my jars and lids through a hot wash in the dishwasher, or alternatively fill them with boiling water, dry briefly in a 100°C fan oven, then pour in the sauce and seal. I've never had one go off or even get a spot of mould, which is a serious feat in my house!

FERMENTED CHILLI SAUCE

CHILLIES HAVE LONG BEEN A FAVOURITE PLANT TO GROW AT HOME. Each year when choosing seeds, I spend hours over the chillies, researching exciting varieties, sowing beloved classics and trying a few new experiments. One plant can yield a good thirty chillies, so with the twenty or so plants we grow each year there's a lot to play with. We dry a fair few to make different coloured and flavoured chilli flakes and powders. A lot get eaten fresh in daily cooking, but most find their way into fermented chilli sauce, which is an absolute staple. Fermenting is a form of preservation that uses wild bacteria to create natural acids to preserve food, in the same way that pickling does with vinegar. Fermented foods are great for the gut in that you're introducing healthy bacteria, but they're also healthier than pickles, which use a fair bit of sugar to balance out the harshness of vinegar. Fermenting might sound complicated but it's actually a very easy and free process. Here is a sauce that you can adapt to your own taste, that will last for months if stored correctly.

You can use a few varieties of chilli here for different levels of spice. The bulk of my chillies will be mild, as it's always easy to ramp up the heat with a few Scotch bonnets or bird's-eye chillies. But usually I find it's a case of decreasing the heat by bulking it out with as many red peppers as need be. Nuclear-grade sauce seems pointless to me . . . you can't taste the chilli, let alone what's on your plate.

MAKES I LARGE JAR

1kg red chillies (see above)

6 red peppers

2–3 sweet apples, or try other fruits: pineapple, pear, mango, etc.

a thumb or two of fresh ginger

coriander seeds (optional)

sea salt

cider vinegar, to taste

soft brown sugar, to taste

olive oil, for sealing

Fermenting is all about weight, as this determines the percentage of salt you use. Salt is a natural preservative and in the right quantities creates an environment that lets good bacteria thrive while stopping bad bacteria. The good bacteria live on the sugars in the food and release lactic acid as a by-product, and it is this lactic acid that acts as a pickle and naturally preserves your ingredients.

You need a big bowl. Chop the stems off the chillies and peppers, then cut in half and remove the seeds. Peel and core the apples, then peel and chop the ginger. Add the coriander seeds, if using. You now need to weigh the exact amount of produce you have. Let's say it comes to 2kg, you need 2% of the weight in sea salt, which is 40g. Pour the contents into a food processor, add in the salt and blitz to an even paste. Pour this paste into 1 large or 2 medium jars, really pressing it down to get rid of any air; ideally, you want the mixture to be submerged in its own liquid.

CONTINUED OVERLEAF

Now add a glass fermentation weight to hold the chilli paste down, or a yoghurt pot lid with a boiled stone on top. Gas is produced during fermentation and as chillies have quite a lot of sugar in them they ferment pretty wildly, so make sure there is a good 5cm of room at the top of the jar. Remove the rubber ring from the jar so gas can escape, then close the lid and leave in a cool, dark place to ferment for about a week, pressing down the solid chilli paste into the liquid brine each day – it must be submerged. After a week, have a taste – it should be delicious and wonderfully sour by now. The sourness is proof that fermentation has produced enough lactic acid, which is the preservative. Pour into a high-speed blender, blitz until smooth and have another taste. Add a glug of cider vinegar to help with long-term preservation, then balance out the acidity with a little soft brown sugar. Keep mixing, tasting and adjusting until you have a sauce that you love.

Pour into sterilised jars, then cover with a little layer of olive oil and place in the fridge. I don't pasteurise because I like the good bacteria, but this means the sauce is technically still alive. The fridge will massively slow this down, but don't screw the lids on too tight, so that any gas created can escape. The chilli sauce will now last for months if kept cold in the fridge. Use it on eggs, mixed through mayo, in sandwiches, with barbecues, in sauces, etc. Sometimes a little white mould will appear, but this is nothing to worry about – just scrape it off.

CHICKEN STOCK

It is rare for there not to be a pot of chicken stock gently bubbling on the stove. I make vast cauldrons, too big for the fridge so they sit outside the kitchen door in the cold. We live off the stuff. I love chicken stock for the principle of using something that would otherwise go to waste, for its healing, restorative and nourishing qualities, as well as being a great way to clear out the fridge. I would always recommend using homemade chicken stock if you can. I find the shop-bought stuff (unless really high-quality bone broth) too strong and dominating, and if using would recommend watering it down a little. Here is more of a way than a recipe, as it's a very instinctual thing to make and you should be free with the ingredients you have to hand.

First, you need some chicken bones, and a bit of meat on them is no bad thing for added flavour. The leftovers from a roast chicken are a great way to start but you can also go to your local butcher for a bag of chicken carcasses. You can choose to roast these for a darker and richer-flavoured stock, or leave them unroasted for a lighter stock. If making a risotto or soup for instance, I prefer a lighter chicken stock, which adds depth without taking over the flavour. But if making a ragù, or drinking the broth with noodles etc., I would go roasted for the added oomph.

On to the other ingredients – here is where the fun starts. The first thing to say is that if you put too much of anything in, these ingredients will mask the other important flavours. Too many leek tops and the stock goes very dark and it's all you can taste. Too many carrots, it gets sickly sweet. So be instinctive and find the right balance. I always add a few onions to my stock, a stick of celery, some leek tops and a few bay leaves, but from there, the options are endless.

Any old bits of celery, a squishy tomato, ginger, parmesan rinds, dry bits of ancient chorizo or bacon hiding at the back of the fridge, tired onions, old sprouting garlic cloves, that last shrivelled mushroom, I could go on and on. Use it as an excuse to clear out the fridge. Peppercorns, dried chillies, fennel or bundles of tired old herbs are all good additions as well.

Lastly, of course, is time. A good stock needs time to infuse; leave it at the gentlest of simmers for hours, the longer the better really. Once ready and deeply infused, strain off the stock, then pour it back into the pot. From there, if it is strong enough already, just season and get cooking. But if need be, you can leave it bubbling for a little longer to reduce and intensify in flavour. If you've made a lot, keep it cold or it will sour quickly. We often freeze ours in little Tupperware boxes to be popped out when needed.

BASIC MAYONNAISE & AÏOLI

Homemade mayo couldn't be easier to make and tastes leagues above the shop-bought stuff. Here is a simple velvety and rich mayonnaise, great on its own, but also as the beginning for many other flavoured mayos. This recipe makes 1 good-sized jar. You can halve it if you want but it lasts ages in the fridge and goes with everything. If you don't have a food processor, you can do this with a handheld whisk or immersion blender.

To turn this into aïoli, add two or three more garlic cloves.

> *200ml extra virgin olive oil*
> *200ml sunflower oil*
> *1 whole egg, plus 1 yolk*
> *1 tbsp Dijon mustard*
> *1 large clove of garlic, finely grated*
> *1 hefty pinch of flaky sea salt*
> *juice of 1 lemon*

Mix the two oils together in one pourable container.

Add the egg, yolk, mustard, garlic, salt and half of the lemon juice to a food processor. Blitz well to combine. Once combined, with the processor running, slowly start adding the oil. I cannot emphasise enough how slowly. If the oil is added too fast, the mixture will curdle (separate) and you have to start again. So, while whisking, add the oil in the slightest trickle possible. It will start thickening after a while and make a lovely thwacking noise as it slaps the sides of the blender. This signals that you can pour slightly faster, but don't overdo it.

Once all the oil has been emulsified, add the rest of the lemon (or any other chosen flavourings). Taste, and adjust the seasoning. Use more salt, lemon and mustard to find the balance that works for you.

SALSA VERDE

A classic salsa verde is a key recipe to know. Punchy, bright and packed with verdant goodness, this was the first sauce I ever learnt to make in the restaurant world. It's incredibly versatile and as good with roasted veg as it is meat and fish.

> *50g fresh flat-leaf parsley*
> *10g fresh tarragon, dill or chervil*
> *20g capers*
> *about 5 cornichons*
> *3–5 salted anchovies (optional)*
> *1 tsp Dijon mustard*
> *a tiny splash of red wine vinegar*
> *quality olive oil, but not too peppery or bitter*

Take the parsley, bunch up the leaves, then, with a sharp knife, chop and chop, again and again until it's really fine – I generally chop up the thinner stalks too. Strip the leaves from the tarragon, dill or chervil and finely chop. Rinse the capers and roughly chop (a bit of texture here is great), then do the same with the cornichons. Finally, if using, chop and smush the anchovies into a paste. Put all this into a bowl, along with the mustard, a pinch of flaky salt and the tiniest splash of red wine vinegar. Mix well and, as you're doing so, trickle in olive oil to achieve a loose-ish consistency. Have a taste and add more salt, mustard, vinegar, even a few extra cornichons if you think it needs some added crunch. Salsa verde is a classic example of needing to taste and adjust until you are happy with the balance.

This can be made in advance, but if you're making it the day before, add the vinegar at the time you're going to eat it, as the acidity will take away the green vibrancy. This sauce is fantastic with fish and lamb, stirred through lentils or boiled new potatoes, even mixed through mayo. It's a great thing to know.

HORSERADISH SAUCE

Homemade horseradish sauce is one of the greatest sides there is, I love the stuff. It's leagues above the vinegary version you can buy in a jar. For me, roast beef is incomplete without this glorious condiment and it's particularly incredible with smoked fish and earthy beetroots. It's also unbelievably easy to make so you have no excuse not to. And if you ever have a cold, it clears out the sinuses wonderfully.

> *1 fresh horseradish root*
> *400g crème fraîche*
> *½ lemon*
> *sea salt*

Get ready to cry. Peel the skin off the bottom half of your horseradish root and grate finely until you have 80g. You will wish you had goggles. Combine the horseradish with the crème fraîche, and add a little lemon juice and a generous pinch of sea salt. Mix well and taste to check your seasoning. It should be fiery and fantastic, but be careful with the lemon, you don't need much.

HOMEMADE PESTO

Now there are two ways to make pesto . . . The traditional one, of course, is in a pestle and mortar, from where it gets its name, the other in a food processor, which is speedy and quick. There are merits to both, one being easy, the other keeping traditions alive. I find adding a whole clove of garlic to pesto *completely* takes over and destroys the subtle marriage of flavours. So I use just ¼–½ a clove, grating in more if desired at the end. However, the joy in recipes is that they are just a guide, so use as much garlic and parmesan as you like and get the balance right for you. Pesto can, of course, be made with many other nuts and herbs. Use the technique outlined below in all sorts of wild, imaginative ways.

> *½ clove of garlic*
> *100ml quality olive oil (not too bitter)*
> *120g fresh basil leaves*
> *50g pine nuts*
> *40g parmesan, finely grated*
> *30g pecorino, finely grated*

Put the garlic into a pestle and mortar with a pinch of salt and grind into a paste. Pour in a trickle of the olive oil and add a handful of basil. Grind and bash the basil right down into a paste so that it releases its oils, then add the next handful with another trickle of olive oil until all the basil has been used. Follow with the pine nuts and grind them into the basil – I like to leave mine with a lot of texture, but some prefer them smooth. Finally, stir through the grated parmesan and pecorino, and then the remaining oil. Taste, adjust, pour into a jar and top with a little more oil to stop it discolouring.

If using a food processor, put in the basil, grate in the garlic and pour in the oil. Blitz until completely smooth, then add the pine nuts, parmesan and pecorino and pulse to your desired consistency – I like it quite rough and chunky. Taste, find the balance, then store as outlined above.

SHORTCRUST PASTRY

The simplest pastry of them all. Shortcrust is great for both savoury and sweet tarts, with a crisp, buttery crust and a heavenly texture. The absolute key for pastry is to keep things cold and work quickly; the less time you work the dough the better as this stops gluten forming, which makes it go hard. I use a food processor for ease, but you can easily make this by hand.

for a 25cm tart
200g plain flour
100g chilled butter, cubed
ice-cold water (a splash of cider vinegar is great if making a savoury tart)
1 egg, beaten

Chuck the flour and butter into a food processor and season with a pinch of salt. Pulse for about 20–30 seconds until the butter coats the flour in very fine breadcrumbs. Then, with the mixer running, add ice-cold water a tablespoon at a time until it begins to form into a ball. The second it does, turn the mixer off and bring the dough together in your hands, pressing it into a ball rather than kneading. The less blitzing and water the better. Flatten into an disk about 4cm high, wrap in cling film or baking parchment and chill for 30 minutes.

Remove the pastry from the fridge, flour your surface, place the dough down and flour the top of it too. With a rolling pin, always rolling away from you and turning the dough as you go, roll out the dough into an even disk, around 3mm thick. Take your tart case and hold it over the pastry to ensure it fits. Then flour your rolling pin, place on one third of the pastry and roll the pastry on to it. Then unroll into your tart case. Gently press the pastry into the case, then I take a little smidge of excess pastry and use that to press the dough into the edges. Leave some excess hanging over the sides as this helps stop the pastry from shrinking when it cooks. Prick the base evenly with a fork, which releases any trapped air that would otherwise bubble up underneath the pastry. Place in the freezer for 20 minutes.

Preheat your oven to 180°C fan. Remove the pastry from the freezer, cut a piece of baking parchment a little wider than the tart shell, scrunch it into a ball, then unravel and place on top of the pastry. Fill with blind-baking beans (or dried lentils, beans, rice etc.). Place on a baking tray, slide into the oven and cook for about 20 minutes, until the edges are beginning to go golden. Remove from the oven, then carefully lift out the baking parchment and beans and place back in the oven for a further 10 minutes, until the base is completely cooked, being careful it doesn't take on too much colour. Finally, remove once more, brush with beaten egg and place back in the oven for a minute or so to dry the egg. This seals the pastry, which ensures it stays crisp when filled. And there you have it, blind-baked pastry ready for filling. A bit of a faff, but actually very easy once you get the hang of it.

ROUGH PUFF PASTRY

Puff pastry is very special indeed, but a bit of a mission to make. I usually just buy it ready-made, as the shop-bought stuff is great for many of the flat tarts and pies in this book (make sure to buy the 'all butter' kind). However, there is a cheat's puff pastry that is incredibly delicious, buttery and flaky, and couldn't be easier to make. I highly recommend this for my chicken pie, as well as the apple turnovers.

250g plain flour
1 tsp fine sea salt
200g butter, cubed
150ml cold water
1 egg, beaten

Pour the flour and salt into a large bowl, then follow with the cubed butter. Pour in two-thirds of the water and stir the mix together until it forms a very shaggy dough, you can add more water if you think it needs it. Cover and leave in the fridge for 20 minutes. When ready, lightly flour your work surface, then pour out the dough. Start rolling out the dough into a long rectangle, only working in one direction. The dough should have a marbled butter effect, which is good; try not to work the butter into the dough. Fold the top third of the dough in on itself and then fold the bottom third over that. Then turn it 90 degrees, roll out into a rectangle again and repeat the process twice more. What this does, is stretch out those marbled streaks of butter, creating layers in the dough. When you then cook the pastry, these layers melt and leave air gaps that make the pastry lovely and crisp. When you've finished working the dough, wrap and chill for 30 minutes so it can rest.

To cook, simply roll out the pastry to about 4–5mm thick. Place on your pie, allowing the edges to hang over, brush with beaten egg, cook at 220°C fan for 10 minutes, then turn the heat down to 200°C fan and cook for a further 20–30 minutes, until golden and puffed.

GALETTE PASTRY

Galettes are brilliant free-form tarts that require none of the faff of blind baking. You simply make the tart directly on your baking tray, fold over the edges, brush with egg and whack it in the oven. This pastry recipe was passed on to me by the ever-inspiring Lloyd Morse of the Palmerston in Edinburgh. It is flaky, buttery and biscuity, with a lovely texture and gentle flavour from the cider vinegar. I couldn't recommend it highly enough. I've used a stand mixer here but you can also make this by hand in a large bowl.

> 270g plain flour
> 170g butter, diced small
>   and put in the freezer
> 15ml apple cider vinegar
> 60ml cold water
> 1 egg, beaten

In a stand mixer with the paddle attachment, add the flour, two-thirds of the cold butter and a generous pinch of salt. Turn on and mix until the flour is beginning to look like breadcrumbs. Then add the remaining butter and continue to mix until the mixture looks like breadcrumbs, but with chunks of butter throughout; this is what makes it flaky later on. At this point, add the vinegar and half the water and mix briefly to combine. Now turn the mixer off and push the pastry down against the bowl to see if it comes together as one; if it doesn't, it may need a splash more water. When you feel the mixture is cohesive enough, bring the dough together by pressing it (rather than kneading it, which results in a tough pastry) into a disk about 7cm high, then wrap in baking parchment and allow to rest and chill in the fridge.

After half an hour the pastry is ready to bake. Flour your work surface and roll the pastry out into a disk about 4–5mm thick. By rolling away from you and turning the pastry ever so slightly with each roll, you should get an even thickness all round.

When ready, slide on to a sheet of baking parchment and then on to a baking tray. Top with your filling, leaving a 5–7cm edge all the way round. Then fold over this edge, brush with beaten egg, sprinkle with a little salt and bake at 220°C fan for about 30–50 minutes depending on your filling. The key is that the pastry is golden brown, crisp and flaky.

INDEX

ACKNOWLEDGEMENTS

THIS BOOK IS SOMETHING I'VE BEEN DREAMING OF FOR YEARS, but was terrified to start. The seed was there but I put it off, daunted by the task and never quite feeling ready. I think I saw writing a book as a lonely process that would have me tied to a desk, tapping away for months on end with a looming deadline. And in part I was right, what a challenge it has been, but however hard it was also a time of joy and dedication. The best moments were when our incredible team came together, to cook, grow, taste, plant, discuss and embed ourselves in the daily workings of our little farm. The result is a collection of recipes and stories that I am deeply proud of, but I couldn't have done it alone and I owe my thanks to the many involved.

First to thank are Mum and Dad, who have always been the most supportive parents I could have asked for. From such a young age they saw a passion and allowed me to experiment in their kitchen; bravely swallowing my early concoctions and inventions, gently encouraging, tasting and teaching, and then eventually allowing me to turn their little cottage into a scruffy smallholding. We've been through thick and thin together, learning a new way of life entwined with nature. Thank you for it all, I owe you so much and hope the mess has been worth the joy.

To my brother Joss, who works as my right-hand man. I've been incredibly jealous of you this past year, working outside and tending the farm in all that blazing sunshine while I stared out the window sitting in front of my laptop. We cooked and tasted almost every dish together and I couldn't have done it without your advice and encouragement. Not only that but it was the best year we've had in the garden yet, I don't know what I'd do without you.

To my dear publishers at Ebury. It's a huge team and there are many to thank. But especially Lizzy and Celia; your gentle hand holding, patience and encouragement have been so nurturing, pushing me forwards and spurring me on. I knew I was in the right place from that very first meeting and together we realised and captured the essence of this book. You built the perfect team around me, with so much belief and utter patience to the very end. Thank you for allowing me this opportunity and supporting me as you have.

To my dear managers Alice and KJ, who have been there from the very start. You saw something in me when I was just a wee little ragamuffin exploring the countryside and have helped me realise my dream. Thank you for all the guidance, advice and support over the years – what a journey it's been!

To Elena Heatherwick, who shot this book. Your joy and life force astounds me, what a pleasure you are to work with. We had such fun documenting the year and the way you captured the ethereal nature of the seasons and the food we made is better than I could ever have imagined… thank you for it all. And thanks to Marco Kesseler, who not only assisted Elena, but hand modelled, hair styled, plate chose and ensured that not a morsel went to waste; your appetite is legendary.

So much of a book comes down to the design. And we couldn't have been in better hands than with Julian Roberts. I love the way you carefully considered and crafted the beautiful pages within. You've made it feel like such a warm and peaceful book.

Florence Blair was the mastermind who quietly organised and prepared for our shoot weeks. Without your careful planning and hard work all the fun we had wouldn't have been possible. We couldn't have done it without you.

Leaving London was the best decision I ever made. But it did come with one great sacrifice; I left behind a group of incredible friends. It has been so hard watching you all from afar, and I miss you terribly. I know I've been awful, but I just wanted to say how much I love you all. And to say thanks for your loyalty and friendship despite my absence. Now that this is finished, I vow to be more present.

A huge thanks must also go to all of you who've bought this book and to those that have followed and encouraged me online. Your support and advice over the years has meant the world to me. It can be quite a solitary life at times, which suits me well, but to have you there has always spurred me on.

There is also a great list of friends, neighbours, partners and locals to whom I owe so much. My dear Auntie Lou for your help and encouragement. Jasper for your ever guiding wisdom, friendship and hospitality. Paul 'the wolf' Weaver, my dear head chef, Myles and all those at Noble Rot where my love of cooking became a career. Ellie, your infectious love of cooking, wise advice and support couldn't have come at a better time. Ben Lebus, for your counsel and encouragement along the way. Ben and Alexis, for your laughter and love for this place and what I do. Lucian, for your sharp wit and hard graft, always in full waterproofs! Anaïs, for your years of patience, bottle-feeding, birthing assistance and so much more, thank you for it all. Our farming neighbours, the Rowes, who have been so welcoming and instructive in the matters of hay making and other farming conundrums. Angie and Tor for your wisdom and emergency phone calls in all matters of sheep. Ben and JC for years of help in the veg patch with much laughter and jest over wood chipping, weed pulling and taste testing.

And lastly… to my dear grandparents, but particularly you, Granny. It was you who really started this all and instilled in me a great love for food and cooking. So many of my childhood memories are based around your beautiful home and the food you produced with such flair. Your wicked smile, cheek pinches and charismatic love of life was utter joy to be around. Every stir of the pot and pinch of salt is in honour of you and I can still smell your spice cabinet when I close my eyes. I'm so glad to have had those years with you and wish you were still around to see where it led.

8

Ebury Press, an imprint of Ebury Publishing
20 Vauxhall Bridge Road
London SW1V 2SA

Ebury Press is part of the Penguin Random House group of companies
whose addresses can be found at global.penguinrandomhouse.com

Penguin
Random House
UK

Text © Julius Roberts 2023
Photography © Elena Heatherwick 2023, except photos on
pages 11, 35 and 110, by Julius Roberts
Illustrations © Jethro Buck 2023

First published by Ebury Press in 2023

www.penguin.co.uk

A CIP catalogue record for this book is available from the British Library

ISBN 9781529198997

Design: Julian Roberts
Artworker: maru studio
Photography: Elena Heatherwick
Illustrations: Jethro Buck
Food and Prop Assistant: Florence Blair

1. quote on page 242 from John Steinbeck

Colour origination by Altaimage London
Printed and bound in Italy by L.E.G.O. S. p. A.

The authorised representative in the EEA is Penguin Random House
Ireland, Morrison Chambers, 32 Nassau Street, Dublin D02 YH68.

MIX
Paper | Supporting
responsible forestry
FSC® C018179

Penguin Random House is committed to a sustainable future for our business,
our readers and our planet. This book is made from Forest Stewardship
Council® certified paper.